A Dream Denied

A Dream Denied

INCARCERATION, RECIDIVISM, AND
YOUNG MINORITY MEN IN AMERICA

Michaela Soyer

UNIVERSITY OF CALIFORNIA PRESS

University of California Press, one of the most distinguished university presses in the United States, enriches lives around the world by advancing scholarship in the humanities, social sciences, and natural sciences. Its activities are supported by the UC Press Foundation and by philanthropic contributions from individuals and institutions. For more information, visit www.ucpress.edu.

University of California Press
Oakland, California

Library of Congress Cataloging-in-Publication Data

Names: Soyer, Michaela, 1980– author.
Title: A dream denied : incarceration, recidivism, and young minority men in America / Michaela Soyer.
Description: Oakland, California : University of California Press, [2016] | Includes bibliographical references and index.
Identifiers: LCCN 2016003759 | ISBN 9780520290440 (cloth : alk. paper) | ISBN 9780520290457 (pbk. : alk. paper)
Subjects: LCSH: Juvenile delinquency—United States. | Juvenile delinquents—Behavior modification—United States. | African American juvenile delinquents—Massachusetts—Boston. | African American juvenile delinquents—Illinois—Chicago. | Hispanic American youth—Massachusetts—Boston. | Hispanic American youth—Illinois—Chicago. | Juvenile recidivists—United States.
Classification: LCC HV9104 .S748 2016 | DDC 364.3609744/61—dc23
LC record available at http://lccn.loc.gov/2016003759

Manufactured in the United States of America

25 24 23 22 21 20 19 18 17 16
10 9 8 7 6 5 4 3 2 1

In keeping with a commitment to support environmentally responsible and sustainable printing practices, UC Press has printed this book on Natures Natural, a fiber that contains 30% post-consumer waste and meets the minimum requirements of ANSI/NISO Z39.48-1992 (R 1997) (*Permanence of Paper*).

For Ed Silver, my husband, who believes in me even when I don't

Contents

Acknowledgments

The teenagers and their families who are the topic of *A Dream Denied* deserve the first acknowledgment. The families let me—a stranger at first—into their lives and patiently answered my questions. I am grateful for their trust. I hope they can find some value in my representations.

A first book is really the work of a community of scholars and friends rather than the product of one individual author. *A Dream Denied* developed out of my dissertation research at the University of Chicago. This book would have been impossible without the support of my committee members, Elisabeth Clemens, Bernard Harcourt, and Mario Small. Bernard Harcourt has significantly shaped this book's theoretical framework. It was he who introduced me to Foucault's lectures about the hermeneutics of the self. He continuously engaged with the intellectual and empirical aspects of my work and offered kind encouragement throughout the writing and fieldwork process. Mario Small's class on case study methods inspired the methodological approach I have taken in this book. His critical engagement with early drafts constantly forced me to sharpen and reevaluate my analytical focus and methodology. Elisabeth Clemens guided me through inevitable bureaucratic hurdles of my fieldwork. Without her patience and measured advice I would have not been able to see this project to completion.

I have also been fortunate to have a network of friends and colleagues who commented on multiple versions of this manuscript. I am particularly indebted to Danielle Raudenbush, Gordon Douglas, and Jan Doering, who have been critical readers as I have turned my dissertation into a book. Abigail Ocobock, Dan Huebner, Brian Cody, Naomi Bartz, Lizzy Kate Grey, and Alicia VandeVusse read early versions of my dissertation, and their insights have directly and indirectly shaped this project.

My time in a postdoctoral fellowship at the Justice Center for Research at Penn State University in State College was crucial for reconceptualizing my dissertation as a book manuscript. I would like especially to thank Susan McNeeley, Gary Zajac, and Doris McKenzie for their advice and support.

Over the years I have relied extensively on the friends and family members who were by my side as I worked through the emotional burden of fieldwork and writing. Gawin Tsai and Andrea Leverentz deserve special mention. Andrea has been a mentor, and her thoughtful comments have improved this manuscript significantly. I am also indebted to my parents, who have supported me financially and emotionally through many years of graduate school and beyond. I was able to spend summers in Germany writing while they took care of our two children, Rebekka and Cordelia. My husband, Ed Silver, has patiently carried the biggest emotional burden of my intensive fieldwork and writing process. He has been an interlocutor, a patient friend, and a loving father to our children when I couldn't be there for them. His contribution to my work cannot be overstated. He deserves credit not only for the book's title but also for helping me theorize my empirical observations. I am privileged to have a partner who is a true intellectual and whose intelligence is a constant inspiration.

Finally, I would like to thank Maura Roessner and her editorial team, along with freelance copy editor Steven Baker, who guided me carefully and efficiently through this editorial process.

My dissertation research has been funded by NSF Dissertation Improvement Grant No. 1124430.

Abbreviations

CHINS	child in need of services
CBT	cognitive behavioral therapy
DCF	Department of Children and Family (Boston)
DCFS	Department of Children and Family Services (Chicago)
DYS	Department of Youth Services
IYC	Illinois Youth Center (Chicago, St. Charles)
JDAI	Juvenile Detention Alternative Initiative (Chicago)
JTDC	Juvenile Temporary Detention Center (Cook County)
SGA	Scholarship and Guidance Association
SGD	Spanish Gangster Disciple

Introduction

Tell me
Why should it be my loneliness
Why should it be my song
Why should it be my dream
deferred
overlong

Langston Hughes 1951

When our oldest daughter turned two, my husband bought *The Little Engine That Could* for her. Having grown up in Germany, I had never read the story before. The plot fascinated me. The children's books I grew up with definitely did not include tales of overcoming one's limitations. In the 1980s in Germany *Der Struwwelpeter* was still common reading material. To this day I remember what happens to poor little Suck-A-Thumb: a tailor with a giant pair of scissors storms in, catches him sucking on his thumbs, and cuts both of them off. As I have learned over the years, *The Little Engine That Could* is only one of countless American children's stories that celebrate the "American Dream." Julia Donaldson's *The Snail and the Whale*, for example, teaches us that small creatures can accomplish great things if they just dare to do them. Never let anybody stop you from pursuing your dreams is the motto of Brad Meltzer's picture book about Amelia Earhart's life. From a very early age, American children are taught that it does not matter where you come from; it is what you do that will define your fate.

Despite a widening gap between rich and poor, the narrative of the "American Dream" continues to shape the collective conscience of American society (Durkheim 1965). According to a recent *New York Times* poll, almost two-thirds of Americans believe that it is possible to be born poor, work hard, and end up rich (Sorkin and Thee-Brenan).[1]

At least since Weber's *The Protestant Ethic and the Spirit of Capitalism* ([1904–5] 2002), sociologists have debated how exactly this cultural trope influences American society. Believing that hard work begets success justifies the enormous wealth a select few accumulate. Shamus Khan's recent ethnography (2011) of St. Paul's boarding school in Concord, New Hampshire, for instance, showed how elite educational institutions transform their students' privileged backgrounds into achievement. In her ethnography of a poor Chicano community Ruth Horowitz (1992) observed that the residents continued to believe in the "American Dream" despite their economic and social marginalization. Likewise, Alford Young (2006) countered stereotypes of a "culture of poverty" by showing that the "American Dream" is most vivid in the imagination of the poorest and most isolated men in his study.

A discourse like the "American Dream" mystifies inequalities and legitimatizes the status quo. Narratives or myths are useful additions to overt oppression. They allow rulers to co-opt their subjects and obscure avenues for social change (Lincoln 1989).[2] From a Gramscian perspective, the "American Dream" thus represents a hegemonic discourse that shapes perceptions and actions of the underclass (Hobsbawm 2011, 321–22).

A Dream Denied investigates how the narrative of the "American Dream" operated in the lives of twenty-three young male offenders in Boston and Chicago. This narrative played a prominent role in the imaginations of the teenagers in this study, compensating for the institutional deficiencies of the juvenile justice system and glossing over its internal contradictions (Zimring 2005). Belief in this narrative sustained the young men's redemption scripts (Maruna 2001). It also distracted them from the practical marginalization they confronted as they tried to desist from crime (Pettit and Western 2004; Pager 2003). Without the means to build a new life, they derived from the "American Dream" narrative only a meager placeholder for more concrete strategies of action.

Social scientists have described the juvenile and criminal justice systems in the United States as entities that control an already subjugated and impoverished population (A. Goffman 2014; Alexander 2012; Rios 2011). My research extends beyond this consensus to demonstrate how the systems in Boston and Chicago reinforced the teenagers' marginalized social positions in subtle and covert ways. These agencies were not an unequivocally negative force in the lives of the young minority men I worked with. The judicial system was often the only governmental organization providing even nominal support for inner-city children and their families. Without their probation officers, the teenagers were at greater risk of slipping through the cracks of an underfunded social welfare system. In their interactions, both juvenile justice professionals and the offenders they administered relied on the "American Dream" narrative to render meaningful these young men's behaviors within a structural framework that both encouraged and inhibited their successful reentry into society.

INSTITUTIONAL STRUCTURE

Juvenile justice is a bureaucratic system that operates according to an instrumental-rational logic. The organizations in Boston and Chicago were inherently incapable of building mutuality and trust between juvenile justice workers and juvenile offenders. The power imbalance between service providers and clients, combined with the inability to make decisions on an individual basis stifled efforts to help struggling youths. This organizational logic defeated probation officers and juvenile offenders alike (Weber 1979; Blau 1984). As an institution conceived to simultaneously punish and rehabilitate, juvenile justice also ineffectively implemented both aspects of its mission (Zimring 2005). Rehabilitative goals were impossible to achieve within a structure designed to punish and discipline. At the same time, it was also difficult to control juvenile offenders while they were enrolled in rehabilitative programs. Moving beyond the obvious dysfunctions of the US criminal and juvenile justice system is a necessary analytical step. High incarceration rates, discrimination, and racial profiling are incomplete representations of the multifaceted social reality of Latino and African American youths. To uncover the mechanisms reinforcing marginalization of minority youths, I scrutinize the cultural assumptions that frame juvenile justice interventions on a daily basis.

AGENCY

To operationalize how the narrative of the "American Dream" impacted the lives of the teenagers I interviewed, I focus on the concept of agency, specifically on the difference between the agency the teenagers desired or perceived themselves to have and the agency they were actually able to exercise. From a sociological perspective, believing that social barriers can be overcome by hard work is equivalent to assuming that agency trumps structural limitations. The teenagers saw themselves as superagents. Modern sociological theorists have suggested that structure and agency are an interdependent dyad (Sewell 1992; Bourdieu 2001). Sewell argued that social structures constrain or empower an agent depending on their specific configuration. An agent is also capable of influencing and changing the social structure that surrounds him or her. To effect social change, an actor has to activate cultural schemas and resources, two mutually reinforcing entities: resources can support application of cultural schemas, and cultural schemas can help the actor to access resources (Sewell 1992, 27).

The juvenile offenders I observed also interacted dynamically with the structure of the juvenile justice systems in Boston and Chicago. As creative agents they found ways to act autonomously even as they were on probation or held in juvenile justice facilities (A. Goffman 2014; Fader 2013). At the same time, they had to make choices within the parameters that juvenile justice imposed on them. Especially during their incarceration teenagers began to see the world through the eyes of those who supervised them (Mead 1969). Hence, the cultural schemas they activated to make sense of their situation reflected narratives perpetuated by staff members, social workers, and probation officers.

DESISTANCE AND RECIDIVISM

While *A Dream Denied* situates juvenile delinquency within the broader context of inequality in American society, the teenagers' process of desistance and recidivism is an important focus of this book. Agency has long been identified as a crucial part of the desistance process, but it still remains undertheorized in the criminological literature (Sampson and Laub 2005; Giordano et al. 2002). I argue that positive experiences of agency are necessary for successful juvenile justice interventions and eventual desistance from crime. If we understand agency as being able to actively construct one's life (Laub and Sampson 2003, 281), many of the teenagers who participated in this study experienced agency only when they engaged in criminal behavior. The young men were very limited in the choices they were able to make—not only because of their age but also because of the abject poverty that shaped their lives. Paradoxically, the teenagers most explicitly adopted the rhetoric of the "American Dream" while their agency was restricted to small acts of defiance or cognitive disengagement (Fader 2013; Scott 1987). Imagining themselves as super-agents compensated for their inability to act creatively in terms of the nondeviant self they wanted to adopt.

In his later work, Foucault described retreating into the self and discon-necting from the environment as "taking care of the self" (Foucault 2005, 49). The teenagers I interviewed often resorted to "taking care of the self" while they were exposed to juvenile justice interventions. Regardless of the form of punishment they received, they were always able to make choices about the extent to which they allowed the system to infiltrate their being. Yet, as Foucault also noted, true self-transformation is possible only if it is fostered by a noninstrumental relationship to one's surrounding. In fact, a person who wants to take care of his self can often do so only with the sup-port of mentors who surround him (58–59).

The teenagers in Boston and Chicago, in contrast, were mostly on their own as they tried to develop a new identity. This transformation therefore often lasted only briefly. Attempts to desist from crime faltered when they were based solely on following rules and exercising self-control. Teenagers who were successful in the long term "owned" their desistance. They found a job they enjoyed and kept it. They became engaged in sports and art because it validated their talents, or they excelled in school because they saw the positive results of their work. Their choices and the rewards the young men received made it worthwhile for them to stay away from the streets and to continue building a nondeviant self.

Exercising agency productively during the desistance process therefore entails more than just being able to control oneself in the face of temptations and power structures (Gottfredson and Hirschi 1990). It means pursuing self-directed avenues of identity development that allow for positive experiences of self-worth and success beyond the streets (Erikson 1994). Taking the teenagers' desire to create their own "American Dream" seriously has concrete implications for juvenile justice interventions. Rather than curtailing opportunities for engaging in criminal activity, it is necessary to create opportunities that allow young men to experience themselves as creative agents in terms of their new, nondeviant self.

OVERVIEW OF THE BOOK

A Dream Denied connects offending cycles of inner-city teenagers to normative assumptions about success and failure in American society. This book uses the case of two juvenile justice systems to demonstrate how implicit cultural schemas shape the perception and engagement of individual actors with their social environment. Each chapter covers a different aspect of how juvenile justice institutions impacted the teenagers' expectations and subsequent strategies of actions. The teenagers' firm belief in their own agency and their desire to become part of the middle class anchors their pathways in and out of crime to a general debate about inequality, reproduction of disadvantage, and race relations in American society.

Chapter 1, "The Role of Agency in the Desistance Process," connects the "American Dream" narrative to the teenagers' cycles of desistance and recidivism. The rhetoric of the "American Dream" generated unrealistic expectations about the ability to desist from crime. While most teenagers wanted to believe that they could act creatively in terms of their new self, the reality of their daily life was bleak and did not offer any opportunity for experiencing self-worth and success. The concepts "imagined desistance," "automatic desistance," and "creative desistance" capture this discrepancy between theory and practice in the reentry process. Describing how the teenagers moved from imagined to automatic or creative desistance emphasizes that desistance begins as a cognitive process. This imagined desistance is most likely sustained if the new, nondeviant self is formed in relation to prosocial experiences of creative agency.

Chapter 2, "Two Cities, Two Systems, Similar Problems: Juvenile Justice in Boston and Chicago," introduces the teenagers in this study and provides a précis of the structural conditions of juvenile justice at both field sites. I take a comparative approach and demonstrate the great variation of policies and practices between Boston and Chicago. The two systems are contextualized within historical and contemporary developments of juvenile justice in the United States. Despite their differences, both juvenile justice systems are inherently ambivalent, pulled between two different institutional missions: to provide social welfare and to administer punishment (Zimring 2005, 2007b).

Chapter 3, "Too Little Too Late: Juvenile Justice as a Social Service Provider," focuses on the youths' experiences of the punitive and rehabilitative aspects of juvenile justice. This chapter explores the contemporary argument about the juvenile justice system as part of a "youth control complex" (Rios 2011). Inner-city youths were not necessarily subjected to an encompassing police state. In fact, teenagers not classified as "high-risk" for reoffending remained unsupervised and without access to the social welfare aspects of juvenile justice. Regardless of their level of supervision, the teenagers were struggling to gain control over their lives. Those selected out of the system and sent back into their neighborhood without any guidance were unable to experience genuine autonomy because of structural deprivation. This chapter contextualizes depictions of inner-city men as being subject to top-down control mechanisms within a range of alternatives. Left without any support from the juvenile justice system, these youths experienced the poverty and violence that plagued inner-city neighborhoods to be as limiting as constant supervision and control.

Chapter 4, "The Imagination of Desistance," develops the concept of "imagined desistance." This construct is formulated to account for the observation that all the young men who participated in this study were convinced that they would not be rearrested after their initial stay at a detention facility. These narratives of change symbolized the teenagers' strong commitment to the idea of the "American Dream."

For the young men I interviewed, detention centers were the first stop on a winding road that led them through many different juvenile justice institutions. Without their usual distractions, many teenagers began to reflect on their past. Incarceration triggered a desire to build a life away from the streets. Imagined desistance encapsulated their confidence in an American meritocracy and their own ability to turn their lives around. The institutional structures of juvenile justice encouraged teenagers to frame their incarceration as a positive turning point, but did not adequately prepare young men to create a nondeviant identity built on positive experiences of an alternative self. On the contrary, the punitive framework of incarceration restricted young men's ability to exercise agency in relation to their desired nondeviant identity. Consequently, they were unable to develop viable strategies of action that could sustain desistance after their release.

Chapter 5, "Weak Ties—Strong Emotions: Caring for Juvenile Offenders in Boston and Chicago," investigates interactions between teenagers and juvenile justice officials. As these teenagers moved from detention centers into more permanent placements and finally back home, they came in contact with many different representatives of the juvenile justice system. These encounters provided the most important input for how the young men conceptualized their future. Yet the interactions with staff members, clinicians, and probation officers either were fleeting or were shaped by power imbalance and mistrust. Honesty, reciprocity, and properly therapeutic relationships were therefore nearly impossible to achieve in a carceral setting. Youths overestimated their own agency because they had scarcely anything else to hold on to. Even as they were embedded in a network of social workers, clinicians, and regular staff members, the young men realized that these connections were temporary and would not translate into sustained support in the outside world.

Chapter 6, "The Uncertainty of Freedom: Teenagers' Desire for Confinement and Supervision," examines the paradox that some teenagers experienced supervision and control as a positive force in their lives. After their release from juvenile justice facilities, many teenagers had to wear ankle bracelets and were supervised by probation officers or caseworkers. Ankle bracelets, in particular, are uncomfortable and stigmatizing and severely limit the teenagers' mobility. Nevertheless, several young men welcomed the constant control an ankle bracelet or a committed probation officer provided. In fact, being able to stay away from crime was, in their view, closely connected to knowing that transgressions were punished immediately. Many youths in this study had never experienced success outside juvenile justice facilities. Being controlled was not only familiar; it made life predictable, providing clear and attainable goals around which to structure behavioral choices. Embracing supervision conflicted with their narrative of agency and self-reliance. On the other hand, it allowed the teenagers to negotiate a volatile environment and to go through a manageable process of rehabilitation without confronting persisting and disempowering structural forces.

Chapter 7, "'I know how to control myself': Autonomy in the Desistance Process," juxtaposes two cases from Boston and Chicago of teenagers who successfully desisted with those of two teenagers from both cities who recidivated. I offer an in-depth account of the daily struggles the teenagers went through as they were trying to reintegrate into their neighborhoods. Relying on Michel Foucault's lectures published as *Hermeneutics of the Subject* (2005), I introduce a distinction between "creative desistance" and "automatic desistance." These concepts describe different strategies of action that develop in response to specific structural limitations the juvenile justice system imposed. It is important to distinguish between types of desistance in order to understand the limitations of supervision and control in instigating individual change. Teenagers in Boston, for example, engaged in automatic desistance. They defined their individual success or failure in terms of obeying the rules the juvenile justice system placed upon them.

The Chicago teenagers, who were more inconsistently supervised, were able to make creative choices and build a nondeviant identity beyond the parameters of juvenile justice. I argue that managing the youths' need to make autonomous decisions is one of the most important challenges facing contemporary juvenile justice in the United States. Neither juvenile system has succeeded in supporting the teenagers' desire to define a productive self beyond institutional boundaries. The young men I interviewed mainly experienced themselves as creative and autonomous actors when they were selling drugs or robbing people. The juvenile justice system in Boston, in particular, inadvertently tried to redefine the teenagers' expectations of what it means to be successful. For those who engaged in automatic desistance, the American promise of possibility and independence was reduced to the basic achievement of not being incarcerated and to accepting their continuous struggle at the bottom of the social hierarchy.

A Dream Denied challenges the assumption that juvenile justice disempowers minority youth by simply exercising direct control over them. In Boston and Chicago, marginalization of juvenile offenders paradoxically took place through a rhetoric of possibility and success. The narrative of the "American Dream" was so powerful because it distracted teenagers and juvenile justice workers alike from the lack of real opportunities for change. Probation officers, juvenile judges, and social workers were aware of the high recidivism rates and their inability to address socioeconomic factors that put teenagers at continuous risk for criminality. Propagating the idea that disadvantage can be overcome through hard work allowed them to cope with their own failure to make a difference. Finally, the myth of American meritocracy also absolved the juvenile justice system from any long-term responsibility for the youths in their care.

The almost inevitable recidivism affirmed the teenagers' position at the margins of American society. Failing to live up to their exaggerated expectations, they blamed themselves. African American youths, in particular, began to devalue their racial background and cultural heritage. Rather than thinking about their social position in political and historical terms, they internalized a discourse of personal failure. In some cases the young men believed that being controlled was the only way they would ever manage to permanently desist from crime.

Social scientists thus need to shift at least some of their analytical focus from direct mechanisms of control to cultural narratives that rationalize and enable marginalization indirectly. When teenagers want to wear an ankle bracelet because they cannot imagine returning to their community successfully without one, the long-term effects on the social fabric may be as devastating as discrimination visible to everyone. The fact that young minority men cannot see themselves as independently operating citizens tragically demonstrates their exclusion from the "American Dream" they so strongly believe in.

The teenagers I introduce in the following chapters came of age in a society that elected its first African American president. There were no legal barriers preventing them from becoming upwardly mobile. It was easy for the teenagers to believe that they too could be successful if they just worked hard enough. Yet, as the young men tried to desist from crime, they had to realize that the "American Dream" was out of reach for them. This subtly operating hegemonic discourse defeated aspirations and hopes for the future. The teenagers in this case study did not complain, because they blamed themselves and adjusted their expectations to their social position (Haney 2010).

1 The Role of Agency in the Desistance Process

EXPLAINING CRIME AND RECIDIVISM

While they were held in detention facilities or treatment centers, most teenagers expressed an inflated sense of agency. Relying on the cultural narrative of the "American Dream," they believed in their ability to desist from crime, even if the odds were stacked against them. Criminologists often overlook the role agency plays in the desistance process. Structural conditions can be measured and quantified reliably. Operationalizing agency is more difficult. Direct observations of criminal acts are ethically dubious. Even if researchers were able to witness a crime in the making, it would be impossible to generalize from isolated instances. Although agency manifests itself measurably in the social world, it is connected to an internal decision-making process. To uncover motifs and deliberations, criminologists have to rely on in-depth interviews that can only approximate spur-of-the-moment choices. People's predictions or descriptions of their actions are often disconnected from what they are actually doing (Jerolmack and Khan 2014). Given the discipline's focus on applicability and generalizability, it is not surprising that many theories of criminal behavior and desistance focus on structural conditions as explanatory variables (Felson and Cohen 1979; Agnew 1992; Gottfredson and Hirschi 1990).

THE DUALITY OF AGENCY AND STRUCTURE

In contrast to criminologists, sociologists have engaged in countless itera-tions of the agency-structure debate. One of the most influential attempts to theorize agency is Pierre Bourdieu's concept of "habitus." Defined as embodied history, "habitus" shapes our seemingly free choices in style, preferences, and friendships. In *Distinction: A Social Critique of the Judgment of Taste* (1984), Bourdieu describes "habitus" as a socially repro-ductive mechanism that binds the individual, her or his taste, and aspira-tions into a specific class position. Bourdieu's definition of habitus explains impermeable social structures and self-defeating choices (Willis 1981). At the same time, the notion of habitus precludes social change (Joas and Knöbl 2004).

In response to Bourdieu, William Sewell integrates the idea of habitus into a more dynamic model that accounts for actor-driven incremental social change. Sewell (1992) suggests that agency (defined as transposable cultural schemas) and social structure (defined as the distribution of resources) are dialectically intertwined. An actor is equipped with a range of schemata that he can use to modify the social structure he lives in. This decontextualization and reapplication of schemas is the motor for social change. Anne Swidler's concept of a "cultural toolkit" further unpacks the abstract mechanism of schema application. Resonating with Robert Merton's assumption (1938) about crime as an innovative tool to achieve a desired outcome, Swidler (1986) argues that children growing up in dis-advantaged neighborhoods share middle-class values. They have, how-ever, insufficient cultural tools to reach their middle-class goals.

Criminologists who theorize agency draw extensively on these theoreti-cal debates. The advent of life-course research in the mid-1990s has led to a slow integration of theoretical ideas about agency into the empirical world of criminology. Based on retrospective interviews with five hundred former juvenile offenders, Robert Sampson and John Laub, for example, argue that experiencing turning points is important for sustaining long-term desistance from crime (Sampson and Laub 1993; Sampson and Laub 2005). Originally, the influence of turning points on desistance was investigated in terms of single external events that intervene in the life course—for example, marriage (Laub, Nagin, and Sampson 1998) or employment (Uggen 2000). In response to critics, however, Laub and Sampson began to take creativity and agency seriously. They now argue that turning points unfold their transformative potential only if an individual creatively shapes his or her future by acting in terms of the opportunities that have opened up (Sampson and Laub 2005).

Likewise, Peggy Giordano, Stephen Cernkovich, and Ryan Rudolph's work (2002) has been groundbreaking in operationalizing the role of agency during the desistance process. In their study of female offenders, they argue that a series of cognitive shifts in relation to structural "hooks for change" (for example, a new job opportunity) allowed some women to establish a life beyond their criminal past. They emphasize the importance of "agentic moves" for sustaining a life without crime (992). Thus, individual change is not only a reaction to environmental circumstances. The social environment may provide the "scaffolding" for self-transformation, but "individuals themselves must attend to these new possibilities, discard old habits, and begin the process of crafting a different way of life" (1000). Giordano, Cernkovich, and Rudolph therefore explicitly presuppose that the individual who seeks to transform him- or herself needs to have at least a minimal amount of choice concerning the future and should also be able to command a certain amount of power over his or her social environment (999).

Building on Giordano, Cernkovich, and Rudolph's theory of gradual cognitive shifts, Barry Vaughan describes the process of identity development as based on the actor's choices about what kind of person he or she strives to be. Vaughan (2007) suggests that perceptions and judgments of others play an important role in whether or not an individual is able to conceive of a viable new self. Interacting with a new partner, for instance, may provide specific experiences that allow the former offender to develop a concrete idea of what a life without crime could look like (401). Following Paul Ricoeur, Vaughan emphasizes that potential desisters need to narrativize their lives to bridge the gap between past and future selves (396). Much like Maruna (2001), Vaughan (2007) therefore suggests that establishing continuity between one's old and new self through narrative is important for successful desistance from crime. Likewise, Christoffer Carlsson (2012) maintains that through turning points may be distinct events, they are deeply embedded in nonlinear social processes. Emphasizing the interdependence of turning points and broader social mechanisms, Carlsson observes that self-transformation becomes possible through past experiences relating to current events, which in turn can lead to cognitive reconceptualization of the self. Those cognitive changes may then allow for future behavioral change (12).

CRIMINOLOGY AND THE AMERICAN DREAM

Meyer R. Schkolknick was born in South Philadelphia in 1910, the second of two children born to first-generation Jewish immigrants from Poland. Meyer grew up in a slum filled with other newcomers from Europe. Just like their neighbors from Italy and Ireland, his parents had left their native country for a better life in the United States. Meyer's father, who never lost his thick Slavic accent, worked as a carpenter and truck driver. In the meantime his son became enmeshed in the violent life of the neighborhood. "I was a good and loyal gang member," Meyer recalled several decades later. He and his friends threw rocks and empty bottles at their rivals. He could easily have ended up in one of the infamous reform schools that mushroomed in the early 1900s. Fortunately, Meyer, a highly intelligent boy, was able to take advantage of educational pathways that incrementally opened up for talented Jewish students.

By 1961, when the former Meyer Schkolknick recalled his youth for the *New Yorker*, he had become Robert K. Merton, a distinguished professor of sociology at Columbia University. Merton lived in one of the large Tudor houses in Hastings-on-Hudson and was raising his own family worlds away from the "dingy and decrepit houses" of his youth (Hunt 1961, 54). Merton's upbringing fascinated his colleagues. Paul Lazersfeld, who spent his youth in an upper-middle-class Viennese household, soaked up Merton's stories of growing up in an inner-city slum. According to the *New Yorker*, young Meyer was able to move up the social ladder because he "felt the stirrings of an almost obsessive hunger for learning" (54). From Temple University Merton went on to Harvard, where his academic career began to take off. In the early 1930s, Harvard's student body was white, wealthy, and Protestant. Merton was a poor Jewish student who subsisted mostly on milkshakes and sandwiches. He even distilled his own whiskey. Despite his unusual upbringing Merton seemed to be well liked and made up for his lower-class background through his brilliance and gregariousness. The transformation of Meyer Schkolknick to Robert K. Merton has mythical qualities. As Merton conquered the ivory tower, he turned his impoverished upbringing into a classic American success story.

Given his biography, it is perhaps not surprising that Merton became the first sociologist to describe criminal behavior as an innovative adaptation by those who have been excluded from achieving mainstream success. In "Social Structure and Anomie" (1938) Merton understands criminal behavior as an outcome of a dysfunctional society that isolates the less fortunate. According to Merton, a criminal desires normative success just like any well-adjusted, law-abiding citizen. However, for those who come from a disadvantaged social background, conventional avenues to success may be blocked. As a result, the excluded resort to criminality as an innovative strategy to achieve their goals. As Merton (1938) writes: "The cultural demands made on persons in this situation are incompatible. On one hand they are asked to orient their conduct toward the prospect of accumulating wealth; on the other hand they are largely denied effective opportunities to do so institutionally" (679).

At Harvard Robert Merton crossed paths with another Jewish student, Albert Cohen, who was eight years his junior. Both studied under Talcott Parsons, but Cohen also became one of Merton's students. Like his teacher, Cohen (1955) believes that delinquency results from a disconnection between the American promise of unlimited opportunity and the reality of social closure. Cohen, who spent his entire career at the University of Connecticut, died in November 2014 at the age of ninety-six. His obituary, published in the official newsletter of the American Sociological Association, described his struggles in getting admitted to a graduate program, despite his Harvard BA. One department he applied to informed him that they did not admit Jews. Cohen, who eventually earned a Ph.D. at Indiana University in Bloomington, experienced firsthand the paradox of opportunities that are simultaneously present and unreachable—a phenomenon he later identified as the origin of delinquency.

In his seminal book *Delinquent Boys: The Culture of the Gang*, Cohen argues that young men subscribe to a delinquent subculture because it allows them to reach a status and respect they would never acquire within the framework of middle-class culture. A certain degree of social mobility, as well as the relative spatial proximity of the lower and middle classes, encourages the downward dissemination of middle-class norms to the working class. Some people who grow up working class may even be able to climb up the social ladder. They serve as an example of the feasibility of the "American Dream." This possibility of success makes individual failure to achieve upward mobility even more devastating. Subscribing to a subcultural lifestyle that mocks middle-class values, therefore, provides an outlet for this latent aggression. It allows the underdog to feel a sense of belonging, respect, and success.

Cohen and Merton were both outsiders. They epitomized Simmel's stranger—a person who is in a society but not of it (Simmel 1971 [1908]). Their Jewishness marked them as different, even while they had access to the rewards American society bestowed upon its successful members. From a biographical perspective both of them were ideally situated to understand the limitations and possibilities of the "American Dream."

As the twentieth century progressed, theories about anomie, crime, and the "American Dream" fell out of favor. The narrative receded, perhaps because those social scientists who had experienced the complexities of the "American Dream" were now part of the old guard. Or perhaps, as Messner and Rosenfeld (2007) argue, the increase in crime and the cutthroat, neoliberal economic and political climate of the 1970s and '80s marginalized a theory fundamentally concerned with social justice. Regardless of why the theory lost its importance, criminologists moved away from large-scale normative explanations of crime.

In the mid-1990s Steven Messner and Richard Rosenfeld put the "American Dream" again on the agenda. In their book *Crime and the American Dream* (2007) they argue that US society is suffering from widespread anomie—a disintegration of the social fabric that binds the individual to his or her community. In their opinion, this pervasive societal state is responsible for America's exceptionally high crimes rates compared to other industrialized nations.

Echoing Habermas's argument about the colonialization of the life world through the instrumental–rational system world, Messner and Rosenfeld suggest that schools and the family are constantly undermined by economic considerations. Schools, for example, do not foster learning for the sake of learning, but rather prepare their students for entering a market economy. Consequently, Americans favor attachments to the market over any other social institution. Tragically, as American society turns its back on educational, welfare, and government institutions, these institutions also lose their ability to provide an ethical counterbalance to the market economy. Engaging in criminal activities to further one's advancement thus becomes acceptable behavior across all social strata (Messner and Rosenfeld 2007).

In contrast to Messner and Rosenfeld, who develop a general theory of crime, Michelle Inderbitzin (2007a) focuses on the specific manifestation of the "American Dream" narrative in the juvenile justice system. She observes that staff members in juvenile justice facilities utilize the "American Dream" to lower teenagers' expectations of the reentry process. According to the cultural script of starting on the bottom and "pulling yourself up by your bootstraps," the teenagers are encouraged to expect little once they are released. Instead they are counseled to work hard to move up the social ladder. Like Merton, Inderbitzin recognizes that the teenagers' means and ends are disconnected. Aiming low solidifies their position at the bottom of the socioeconomic ladder. Hence, criminal activity seems the only way to achieve upward mobility.

My argument is diametrically opposed to Inderbitzin's observations. I suggest that juvenile justice institutions in Boston and Chicago did not encourage teenagers to "aim low," but rather engendered unrealistic expectations of a smooth and successful reentry process. In Inderbitzin's view, the teenagers are likely to experience a slow crumbling of their expectations over the life course. In contrast, I witnessed a relatively rapid disintegration of the teenagers' aspirations and dreams. Blaming themselves for their repeated failure to desist from crime, their optimism quickly turned into resignation. Believing in their agency, especially in moments when they hardly had any, did not have redemptive qualities (Maruna 2001). Being hopeful also did not increase the teenagers' chances of establishing a nondeviant identity (Abrams 2012). On the contrary, unrealistic expectations facilitated disappointment, hopelessness, and eventually recidivism.

OPPRESSION AND COGNITIVE DISEMPOWERMENT

To understand how the narrative of the "American Dream" disempowered the teenagers in Boston and Chicago, I move beyond the disciplinary boundaries of criminological theories.

Using the example of Appalachian miners, political sociologist John Gaventa (1982) seeks to explain the absence of collective action, despite the presence of grievances and resources for addressing them. Gaventa demonstrates that oppression takes a cognitive toll. Power not only keeps people from fighting back in actual fact but "also influences, shapes, determines conceptions of the necessities, possibilities and strategies of challenge in situations of latent conflict" (15). When the teenagers I interviewed insisted that they can overcome their disadvantage through hard work, or when they told me that they were the only ones to blame for their incarceration, they inadvertently disclosed that they had accepted their current unequal social position as a given. Focusing on this internal process of meaning-making thus reveals that minority teenagers are not simply overpoliced and criminalized. They are also deeply embedded in a hegemonic discourse that presents the United States as an open and meritocratic society.

Gaventa's work heavily draws on a Marxian understanding of ideology. Marx and Gaventa both argue that the inability of the oppressed to see beyond their current social position is a convenient, if not intended, byproduct of extreme structural deprivation (Marx, in Tucker 1978, 158). In contrast to Gaventa's case of capitalist exploitation, the juvenile justice systems in Boston and Chicago did not deliberately marginalize teenagers. In fact, the systems tried to improve the teenagers' lives. However, they lacked the resources to effect meaningful change. To fill this void, the systems perpetuated a rhetoric of self-reliance and responsibility that was disconnected from the social reality the young men faced.

The teenagers' desire to see themselves as independent actors and to narrativize their future in terms of the "American Dream" became a fundamental part of their (imagined) nondeviant identity. Cultural schemata like the "American Dream" have an impact on the social structure that surrounds us. Like any of us, the teenagers in Boston and Chicago acted in terms of their interpretations of their social world. Their ideas about themselves and their social environment were the "switchmen" that shaped their actions (Weber, quoted in Gerth and Mills 1946).

HERMENEUTICS OF THE SELF

The few teenagers who at least temporarily desisted from crime experienced themselves as creative actors in meaningful ways. Their creativity went beyond acting out against a restrictive system. They were able to reap true rewards for their pro-social actions. As a result, their self-transformation was more sustainable and durable. These comparatively successful young men built supportive reciprocal relationships with mentors. They engaged in activities, such as sports, that gave them pleasure and self-confidence beyond the streets. In short, they constructed a new self defined by positive social experiences outside the artificial world of juvenile justice.

Michel Foucault is mostly known for his theory of punishment. In *Discipline and Punish* (1995), he argues that developing efficient methods of control—or, even better, ensuring that disciplined behavior becomes internalized—is economically and politically useful to elites, allowing them to maximize power without paying the true cost of exercising it. Individuals who are disciplined by rigorous timetables, physical exercise, and constant observation are formed into docile bodies. It may therefore seem counterintuitive to draw on Foucault's work to explain the role of reciprocity and choice in the process of self-transformation. Late in his career, however, Foucault conceptually moved beyond his analysis of power structures to develop a theory of the self that distinguishes between temporary reproduction of institutional values and true self-transformation.

Foucault conceptualizes a space beyond the structural mechanisms of discipline that allows the individual to exercise creativity with respect to his identity development. In his lectures at the Collège de France, later published as the collection *Hermeneutics of the Subject* (2005), Foucault

takes the relation of the self to truth as a backdrop for investigating different techniques of the self. What he refers to as "care of the self" was exercised by Greek and Roman philosophers as an act of taking responsibility
for oneself that changed one's way of being in the world. In ancient Greece
this act of purification was often connected to a pedagogical moment, a
discourse—for example, between Socrates and his students. It was a form
of spirituality not geared toward generating knowledge, but designed "for
the subject, for the subject's very being, the price to be paid for the access
to the truth" (Foucault 2005: 15). Foucault contrasts the spiritual "care of
the self" with the post-Cartesian philosophical approach of "knowing
yourself." Knowing yourself, Foucault argues, does not entail a transformation of the subject. It is not possible to gain access to the truth simply
by means of knowledge, contingent on formal adherence to rules of knowledge acquisition. The acquisition of knowledge does not alter the subject's
position in the world; it does not "quiet the soul" (16, 18).

In antiquity, as Foucault observes, the notion of "taking care of one's
self" did not evolve into the rigorous ascetic practices, rituals of self-
denial, and submission to power structures later expressed in Christianity.
Instead of focusing on the outward expressions of piety, the care of one's
self was fundamentally introspective and allowed the subject to become
autonomous within himself. Such transformation was not achieved in a
solitary setting but rather through pedagogical, familial, and friendship
ties as well as love relationships. Taking care of one's self was made possible through relationship with another person (Foucault 2005, 496, 497).
The outcome of taking care of one's self was ideally a new morality that
would be manifested in actions toward the social environment (502). By
taking care of his self, the subject established autonomy in relation to his
environment. Foucault thus conceptually moved away from the power-
and-knowledge axis that leaves no room for autonomous action. In defin-
ing taking care of one's self as an inward mechanism that is outwardly
manifested, he generated a space that allows the subject to operate beyond
power structures and knowledge geared toward "infinite progress."

Like desistance, Foucault's taking care of one's self begins as an internal
process that is later expressed through actions in relation to the social
world. Taking care of the self is a form of submission to social structures
that the self exercises internally and autonomously, supported by disinter-

ested external forces and fundamentally creative in its manifestation. Foucault's concept thus offers us the analytical basis with which to model how agency manifests itself creatively in the desistance process.

I adapt Foucault's autonomous space of taking care of one's self to distinguish between "imagined," "automatic," and "creative desistance." *Imagined desistance,* the first stage of the desistance process, begins while the teenagers are held in secure pretrial facilities. Imagined desistance is an internal process. The young men envision their life without crime on the outside. Encouraged by the artificial and highly structured environment of detention centers or group homes, the teenagers believe that they can overcome their past by simply exercising self-control after their release. Their strategies of desistance are shaped by ideas of disconnection, avoidance, and retreat into their group homes (Leverentz 2014).

In the cases of young men who continue to apply concepts of self-control and obedience after they return to their community, I refer to this type of behavior as "automatic desistance." Teenagers who desist automatically remain successful mostly as long as they are subjected to control mechanisms. They return home in time for their curfew as long as they have an ankle bracelet. Yet, as soon as the constant supervision is loosened, the newly established routines fade away. Their desistance is superficial and highly contingent on external structures of control (Reich 2010). On the surface "automatic desistance" is similar to deterrence. "Automatic desistance" is, however, embedded in the concrete experience of being controlled. While teenagers may be deterred by the abstract knowledge that a robbery can lead to jail time, their "automatic desistance" is facilitated by the control mechanisms they are subject to on a daily basis.

Creative desistance, in contrast, takes place beyond the instrumental-rational relationships fostered by the juvenile justice systems. Creative agency in the desistance process goes beyond the exercise of self-control in the face of power structures. It means connection rather than disconnection from the social environment, and it is the expression of human autonomy. Creative desistance becomes possible when the teenager is able to autonomously employ techniques of the self that may support discipline but are based on pedagogical relationships that the teenager engages in voluntarily. As Foucault (2005) writes, "This work on the self with its attendant austerity is not imposed on the individual by means of civil law or religious obligation, but it is a choice about existence made by the individual. People decide for themselves whether or not to care for themselves" (271).

Differentiating between imagined desistance, automatic desistance, and creative desistance connects the structural interventions of the juvenile justice system to the identity development of the young men in my sample. As I show over the course of this book, the structural conditions of the juvenile justice system are set up to prevent the exercise of creative agency. It is only in moments when the system inadvertently allows for the possibility of taking care of one's self beyond exercising self-control that creative desistance can take place.

This book conceptualizes the utility and necessity of creative agency very differently than recent publications about deviance and crime in the inner city. Alice Goffman and Victor Rios, for instance, focus on deviance as creative self-expression. They describe deviance as an adaptive response to criminalization, constant supervision, and police brutality (A. Goffman 2014; Rios 2011). The teenagers Goffman and Rios studied were aware of their subordinate social position. Rios (2011) even suggests that they engaged in deviance as a form of resistance. In contrast, I witnessed teenagers either not understanding or willfully ignoring their structural limitations. They refused to see themselves victims of racism, poverty, or the juvenile justice system. Nor did the young men make excuses for themselves. Some readily admitted that they committed crimes for the thrill of it (Katz 1988). Most teenagers thought that they were ultimately responsible for the punishment and restrictions they were facing, and they had no doubt that they were in charge of their future. The young men longed to experience themselves as creative actors beyond their life on the streets. My analysis therefore focuses on the ways in which juvenile justice inhibits or enables positive creative self-expression and identity development.

Juvenile justice does not simply criminalize or ostracize youths. Without a doubt, the teenagers I interviewed would rather have avoided the system. Nevertheless, they believed that being held in group homes or detention or treatment centers would ultimately help them to desist from crime. After all, the juvenile justice system was the only government institution that at least attempted to open opportunities for them. In reality, social workers or probation officers did not have the resources to address

the vast social welfare needs of their clients. In the absence of real opportunities they encouraged the young men to believe in themselves and their
superhuman ability to desist from crime. By promising a better future
without opening up avenues for change, juvenile justice inadvertently
reproduced the hegemonic discourse of the "American Dream."

CONCLUSION: SELF-FULFILLMENT AND DESISTANCE

The narrative of the "American Dream" was a meager placeholder for
effective rehabilitation. This cultural trope distracted juvenile offenders
and juvenile justice employees from the facts of failing infrastructure, limited economic opportunities, and racism. It allowed teenagers to feel
momentarily optimistic. Believing in a bright future eased the emotional
burden of incarceration. Unfortunately, the reality that unfolded after the
teenagers were released was complex in ways they were unprepared for.

The young men often could not find anything that would fulfill their
desire to act autonomously and creatively in terms of their own future.
The juvenile justice system in both cities was structurally incapable of fostering the kind of open-ended, mentoring relationships that could encourage a durable identity transformation. At its best, juvenile justice took
care of the teenagers' basic needs. While they were incarcerated, the
youths had their own bed to sleep in. They were safe and not at risk of getting caught up in a shoot-out. Caseworkers and probation officers made
sure the teenagers received clothing vouchers after their release. In Boston
the youths even had access to therapeutic interventions that were supposed to address complicated family situations. Yet, even if being involved
with juvenile justice was a net benefit for some, it was not enough to enable long-term desistance. Being held in juvenile detention facilities did
not teach teenagers how to stay away from crime in a complex environment that would inevitably draw them back to their old life. Most youths
realized fast that school was still boring, that committing crimes was still
fun, and that simply staying in the house and watching TV could not make
up for the excitement of the streets they were trying to leave behind.

At the same time, being part of the juvenile justice system was their
only option for escaping a vicious cycle of poverty and crime. *A Dream*

Denied is thus not an indictment of the juvenile justice system. On the contrary, I believe that the data I collected support increased financial investment in the juvenile justice system. Currently, the juvenile justice systems in Boston and Chicago cannot achieve the various and contradictory goals they are supposed to achieve. It is impossible for one underfunded government institution to fulfill the multifaceted welfare needs of inner-city teenagers while also controlling their behavior (Zimring 2005). Probation officers and caseworkers cannot win the uphill battle against decades of infrastructural neglect and family dysfunction. In the presence of resource deprivation, it is understandable that both teenagers and juvenile justice workers perpetuated the narrative of the "American Dream." Utilizing this myth, however, fostered unrealistic expectations and distracted from the need to create true opportunities for self-fulfillment in the lives of young inner-city men.

2 Two Cities, Two Systems, Similar Problems

JUVENILE JUSTICE IN BOSTON AND CHICAGO

In the fall of 2009, when I visited the Cook County Juvenile Temporary Detention Center (JTDC) in Chicago for the first time, I was not sure what to expect. I had read about the abuse, overcrowding, and unsanitary conditions that led to an ACLU lawsuit filed against the center in the late 1990s. Would I see teenagers living in filth under deplorable circumstances, or had conditions truly improved since Earl Dunlap, a widely respected juvenile justice reformer, took over the JTDC as transitional administrator in 2007?

Unlike, for example, Chicago's Cook County jail, the JTDC did not seem to have been constructed for detaining people. From the outside the building appeared more like an ordinary administrative complex that could stand some renovation. I entered the JTDC as a volunteer for the Kolbe House, a Catholic organization whose volunteers visited the detention center twice a week. The Kolbe House volunteers split up and walked around the floors of the facility fairly unconstrained. Often the teenagers just banged on the glass windows that separated their unit from the hallway to get our attention and to encourage us to visit them. Volunteers were usually allowed to enter the unit to talk to the young men without further scrutiny.

I saw that the conditions were not as bad as I had feared. The teenagers' living quarters were clean. During the day they could walk around freely in their unit. The atmosphere seemed cordial, sometimes even friendly. Teenagers joked with staff members, watched TV, and played card games, and some units had a Ping-Pong table.

Without doubt, the situation at the JTDC had improved significantly over previous decades. At the end of the 1990s, Chicago joined the Juvenile Detention Alternative Initiative (JDAI), organized by the Annie E. Casey Foundation. Cook County was one of the first jurisdictions to participate and is now considered a model site that exemplifies the JDAI's success.[1] The number of children held pretrial in the Chicago JTDC was in 2010 the lowest it had been in thirty years. In 1998 the daily average population was 620; in 2010 it was down to 325. As alternatives to detention, teenagers are now placed on electronic monitoring or sent to secure group homes.[2] Nevertheless, the JDAI's success is only one piece of a complex development.

As I visited the detention center more regularly, I began to notice broken Plexiglas doors while I made my way from one unit to another. Inmates had smashed doors that separated their rooms from the common area. What must have happened in fits of rage was a quiet testimony to the desperation that continued to persist amid the games, noisy conversations, and movies that filled the air in most units. Father Dave Kelly, the chaplain of the juvenile detention center, has been working with incarcerated children for decades. On my first day as volunteer I was allowed to walk around with him. He talked to the young men about their lives. Some of the youths asked for prayers, and others handed over small paintings or poems they had written. Those poems were later circulated in a magazine called *Making Choices*, published by the Kolbe House. In April 2013, the following poem, written by a JTDC inmate, appeared in the thin black-and-white magazine:

Hope

Hope I never die,
Hope I forever last through the
mistakes I made in my past.
Hope I am not misunderstood hope
this nightmare goes by fast.
I look out of my window and see birds

flying pas[t],
with no worries and all their freedom
they have.
Locked in this room that has been
used before.
So freedom less and so hurt,
hopefully the gods and good karma
will be on my side.
cuz' I am not a piece of dirt.

The poetry in *Making Choices* often reflects on mistakes made, hopes for the future, and the current pain of having lost one's freedom. Although some teenagers would refer to the JTDC as "baby jail"—easy to handle in comparison to an adult environment—it undeniably caused suffering as well. The declining pretrial detention rates did not ease the situation of the teenagers who remained incarcerated in the JTDC. Likewise the question of whether or not juvenile justice is ultimately a punitive or rehabilitative experience for teenagers is difficult to answer definitively.

HISTORICAL DEVELOPMENT OF JUVENILE JUSTICE IN THE UNITED STATES

Since its inception, juvenile justice has struggled with its dual mission of supporting and simultaneously punishing children. The early juvenile courts were built on principles reaching back to the so-called houses of refuge established in the first half of the nineteenth century. These institutions were supposed to be a last resort for abandoned, orphaned, and neglected children (Rothman 2008). Relying on the legal principle of parens patriae— the state's right to intervene in family affairs—houses of refuge took control of children whose parents had failed to supervise and educate their offspring (Feld 1999). Taking children out of their family environments was supposed to be an act of charity that would enable them to develop into productive citizens. Over time these well-intended institutions began to morph into precursors of the modern prison. In the second half of the nineteenth century, houses of refuge were mainly supposed to instill obedience and respect for authority in unruly juveniles (Rothman 2008).

By the 1870s, rapid urbanization generated growing social welfare needs. The problem of juvenile delinquency increased substantially, and juvenile justice advocates recommitted themselves to the ideal of parens patriae. The social reformers saw delinquent children as victims of their deplorable circumstances and unfortunate biological heritage. At the end of the nineteenth century the so-called child-savers fiercely advocated for removing delinquent children from their families and sending them to reformatories (Platt 1977).

The child-saving movement culminated in 1899 in the foundation of the first juvenile court in Cook County, Illinois. The court was supposed to be an institution that helped struggling children rather than punishing them (Zimring 2005). George Herbert Mead (1918), an active supporter of juvenile justice, even believed that the juvenile court reframed the hostile human impulse to punish the criminal into a desire to combat social ills (598). A contemporary of Mead, federal judge Julian Mack (1909), proposed that juvenile justice should not punish but rather "uplift" young people who have erred in their ways. (107). Yet, just like houses of refuge, the juvenile court fell short of its rehabilitative ideals. Sentencing was defined by the child's offense rather than by his or her social welfare needs (Platt 1977; Feld 1999; Schlossman 2005; Rothman 2008).

Legal scholars maintain that the stark contrast between rehabilitative rhetoric and punitive practice in juvenile justice systems continued at least until the US Supreme Court enforced the establishment of due process standards in 1967. The decision handed down in *In re Gault* restrained the leeway exercised by juvenile justice judges, who previously had been guided solely by the court's vague mission of reforming and supporting children in need. After *In re Gault*, lawyers were supposed to be present during court proceedings, and the process of judging juveniles began to resemble its adult counterpart more than the social welfare agency the "child savers" had in mind (Feld 1999; Zimring 2005). Unsurprisingly, while *In re Gault* provided judicial protection for underage offenders, it also led to criminalization of teenagers. By the end of the 1990s, Feld argues, punitive tendencies had nearly obliterated rehabilitative efforts (Feld 1999; see also Zimring 2005 and Kupchik 2006).

Perspectives on the current state of juvenile justice mostly affirm the dominance of punitive tendencies amidst an official commitment to rehabilitation. In her study of a maximum security facility, Michelle Inderbitzin (2007b) confirms that juvenile justice personnel are torn between conflicting tasks of punishment and rehabilitation. She acknowledges that staff members try to build meaningful relationships with teenagers, but she also observes a rhetorical emphasis on accountability and punishment. In his book about a juvenile justice training school, Adam Reich (2010) describes a similar conundrum. According to Reich, teenagers simply perform behaviors the training school mandates. Rehabilitation within juvenile justice facilities mainly translates, therefore, into a temporary submission to power structures.

Disentangling the rehabilitative and punitive tendencies of the two juvenile justice systems I studied is far from straightforward. Numerically and rhetorically, the juvenile justice systems in Boston and Chicago seem to have decisively moved away from traditional forms of punishment by joining the Juvenile Detention Alternative Initiative. Like Chicago, Boston has significantly reduced the number of teenagers held pretrial. Pretrial detention rates in Suffolk County dropped by 20 percent between 2007 and 2008. As a result the Department of Youth Services (DYS) was decreased its pretrial detention capacity from 300 to 250 beds in 2009.[3] Commitment to juvenile prisons has declined significantly in both states as well. In 2001 the state of Massachusetts sent 804 teenagers to secure housing units or prisons. Nine years later the DYS committed only 453 children to so-called treatment facilities. Illinois sent 2,697 youths to state-run juvenile prisons in 2001. In 2010 juvenile prisons in Illinois housed only 1,533 inmates.[4]

These numbers not only reflect declining rates of juvenile offending but also indicate that rehabilitation is en vogue again in both cities. My observations confirm a similar trend in both cities: rehabilitative programs have become staples of group homes, detention centers, and prisons, as well as part of probation and parole requirements.

ORGANIZATIONAL STRUCTURE OF JUVENILE JUSTICE IN BOSTON AND CHICAGO

The DYS in Massachusetts is careful to publicly emphasize its rehabilitative approach to juvenile justice. In its 2009 annual report, the DYS asserts that its core institutional values are "engagement with DYS youth by caring, responsible adults, emphasis on pro-social development; building life skills and social competencies; community connection; service access; and support and supervision."[5] The Department of Juvenile Justice in Illinois officially embraces a rehabilitative rhetoric as well. Based on the assumption "that youth have different needs than adults," the department's website states, "youth committed to the department's care will receive individualized services provided by qualified staff that give them the skills to become productive citizens."[6] The Cook County Juvenile Probation and Service Department subscribes to a similar mission. Its goal is "to provide individualized assessments to rehabilitate and prevent further delinquent behavior through the development of educational, vocational, social, emotional and basic life skills which enable youth to grow and mature."[7]

This rehabilitative rhetoric is, at least to a certain extent, disconnected from the fragmented and contradictory organizational structure of juvenile justice in both cities. The juvenile court system of Cook County has two divisions: juvenile justice and child protection. The juvenile justice division hears delinquency cases, including misdemeanors, drug addiction, and truancy. The child protection division, on the other hand, is responsible for hearing any case involving child abuse or neglect and the termination of parental rights.[8]

In practice, these two divisions are closely interrelated. One-third of the Chicago cases were simultaneously assigned to the child protection and juvenile justice divisions. Of the fifteen teenagers whom I followed in Chicago, two were already under guardianship of the state when they enrolled in the study. Both of them lived with relatives. In three cases the custodial rights of parents or other relatives were terminated over the course of the observational period. In these three instances, the main caregiver had refused to take the teenager back into the home because of his criminal behavior. All five teenagers who were under guardianship of the Department of Children and Family Services (DCFS) were assigned caseworkers who made decisions about their placement and the social services they were supposed to receive.

In Boston, decisions about the termination of parental rights because of abuse and neglect are made by the Probate and Family Court Department.

The juvenile court system handles delinquency cases and "child in need of services" (CHINS) cases.[9] Teenagers who had a CHINS case were assigned a Department of Children and Family (DCF) caseworker. Two of the eight teenagers in Massachusetts became involved with the DCF because their parents had filed a CHINS case. As a result, both teenagers were temporarily placed in a group home.

DCFS involvement in Chicago and CHINS cases in Boston demonstrate the coexistence of retributive and restitutive impulses in the juvenile justice system. Although teenagers in Boston are labeled as "in need of service," taking advantage of the services offered is court ordered and mandatory. The teenagers were placed in a group home and had to participate in therapeutic interventions. Obeying the rules of the house and adhering to curfews were obligatory for the teenagers if they wanted to return home. The DCF worker assigned to the cases evaluated the teenagers' progress on a regular basis, and depending on the level of compliance, the time the young men could spent in their family home was decreased or increased.

For the Chicago teenagers involved with the DCFS, the termination of parental rights was permanent and there were no provisions made for them to return home. Although the DCFS in Chicago, like the DCF in Boston, is an agency whose formal mission is securing children's welfare, it was at times difficult to draw the boundary between punitive measures and provision of social services. Initial placement in the DCFS, for instance, often took place because of the teenager's criminal behavior and the guardian's unwillingness to let the child return home. The entanglement of punitive and welfare measures is also exemplified by the fact that some DCFS-involved teenagers had to remain at the JTDC for a prolonged period, not because of their criminal cases but because the child-protection division could not find placements that would allow them to be released.[10]

As the teenagers made their way through the system, they passed through the different administrative branches of juvenile justice. They were held in pretrial detention centers or in group homes. Some were sent to juvenile prisons, or "treatment centers," as these institutions are called in Massachusetts. After their release all teenagers had to adhere to their probation or parole requirements. Juvenile justice in Boston and Chicago was a complex network of public and private institutions whose interventions were rehabilitative in some aspects and punitive in others.

Pretrial Detention

The Chicago teenagers' main experience of incarceration was being held at the JTDC in downtown Chicago. Any juvenile picked up by the police on a warrant is brought to the detention center. While some of the inmates are released after a few days or weeks, others are confined at the JTDC for years while awaiting adjudication. When I volunteered at the JTDC, the teenagers were distributed over three different floors. Each floor contained alphabetically organized units. Every unit was located behind secured walls—high glass windows that made it possible to observe the whole unit from the outside. Although the structure seemed to be designed to maximize the staff's ability to monitor the teenagers' behavior, the JTDC more closely resembled a chaotic conglomeration of youths in jumpsuits than a fine-tuned disciplining institution.

Many times during my visits as a volunteer for the Kolbe House, the high level of noise in the units made it difficult to engage in conversations. During my visits between fall 2009 and spring 2011, the facility began to make efforts to separate juveniles who were tried as adults from the regular population, but it was not unusual that a gang-involved teenager accused of multiple murders was located in the same unit as a young man arrested for a violation of his probation requirements.

The juveniles were allowed outside their rooms most of the day, and they returned to their rooms at different times in the evening depending on their conduct. As an effort to integrate principles of cognitive behavioral therapy, good behavior was rewarded with longer time outside the room, and points for good behavior could also be used to "buy" candy. At the same time, teenagers could be put in solitary confinement if they instigated fights or were caught with contraband possessions. In this special "mental health" unit, teenagers were allowed to spend only one hour per day outside their cells. I once visited a teenager who was sent there because he had attacked a staff member. I was allowed to talk to him briefly through the locked glass door. Teenagers in my study did not attend school while they were at the JTDC. They could speak with a social worker if they expressed a need to do so.

Twelve of the fifteen boys in the sample were transferred, after a brief stay at the JTDC, to a secure group home called the Saura Center. Established by the JDAI as an alternative program to the JTDC, the Saura Center was run by a private organization called the Heartland Alliance. During their time at the Saura Center the teenagers attended the Healy North alternative school, where I was able to recruit them for my research.[11]

At the Saura Center the teenagers I observed and interviewed participated in group sessions and therapeutic interventions based on cognitive behavioral therapy principles. Teenagers were supposed to stay there for only thirty days, but in some cases—for example, when custody was transferred from the parents to the state—the youths stayed there as long as four months. The building was set up more like a group home than a jail, with rooms rather than cells. Youths were not allowed to leave, but if they were determined to run away, the staff did not stop them. The incentive to remain at the center was high, since it was considered a shortcut to being allowed to return home. If a teenager decided to run, a warrant was issued, which would likely lead to more time in the less desirable JTDC.

The Saura Center staff used a point system to reward good behavior. After a teenager had earned a certain number of points, he was allowed to move to a part of the building called the penthouse, where teenagers were allowed to play on an Xbox. The residents were taken on field trips into the community. Participation in those trips again depended on earning a certain number of points. Getting into fights or disobeying staff members, as well as write-ups at school, were noted and presented in court. If the teenagers did not maintain adequate behavior, they had to return to the JTDC.

In Boston, the young men were located at the Eliot Pretrial Detention Center in Dorchester when they enrolled in my study. The detention center in Dorchester was a much smaller and better-organized facility than the JTDC in Chicago. From the outside the detention center looked like an ordinary jail, with barbed wire surrounding parts of the building and a large metal gate. Like the Saura Center and the JTDC, the Eliot

Detention Center had implemented a system of points and levels. If the residents maintained a certain number of points, they moved up a level and were allowed to stay out of their rooms longer. Teenagers who reached the highest level (4) could order takeout food.

At least two clinicians on staff regularly met with every teenager individually. Other staff members also supervised the young men. The assistant director of the facility engaged the residents in various activities, such as playing basketball. During many of my visits to the facility, the staff-to-inmate ratio was approximately 1 to 4.

Despite its small size, the detention center struggled with enforcing discipline and order among youths. During my time there, one teenager in particular posed an extreme challenge to staff members. The young man was held on adult charges at the facility, having attacked and stabbed a passenger on an MTBA (Massachusetts Bay Transportation Authority) train. The episode was caught on video widely distributed via Boston news media. From the staff's perspective the teenager did not respond to any disciplinary mechanisms. He allegedly instigated fights and was involved in what was referred to as a riot just before Thanksgiving 2011. The facility regularly resorted to solitary confinement to control the youth's behavior—a choice that, in the eyes of other inmates, usually made the situation worse and created more friction between staff and inmates. After the violent incident in November 2011, the young man and several of his suspected accomplices were distributed to different, apparently more secure facilities, only to be returned to Dorchester a few months later.

Treatment Centers and Juvenile Prisons

After their stay at the Eliot Detention Center, the Boston teenagers were either released into the community or committed to the DYS system, which meant they were sent to a treatment facility and assigned caseworkers. Five out of the eight young men in this study were committed to such "treatment centers."

The sentence imposed was based on grid levels ranging from 1 to 6. At the lowest level, commitment to the facility ranged from one to four months. Teenagers assigned grid level 6 could spend up to thirty-six months in DYS custody. Grid levels also determined the type of facility a youth was sent to. Hardware-secure facilities were treatment centers that housed teenagers with grid levels of 4 and above. Staff-secure (described below) or residential placements were accommodations that resembled group homes. Teenagers assigned grid level 1 were placed in the community (DCF group home, foster family, or the family home) after release.[12]

Two young men in this study were held in a hardware-secure facility in Roslindale, officially called the John J. Connelly Youth Center. One teenager had to remain there for fifteen months; the other one was released after thirteen months. The facility bore a strong resemblance to an adult penitentiary. The teenagers themselves were locked behind heavy metal doors in individual cells and had to wear jumpsuits that signified their inmate status. There was a recreational area in which the teenagers could watch TV or play video games.

I interviewed the teenagers in an unused cell that was at times converted to a storage room for contraband recovered during regular searches; sugar packages, spoons, napkins, and food taken from the cafeteria seemed the most common confiscations. When I once ironically remarked that these items seem to be "very dangerous," the staff member accompanying me replied exhaustedly that I had no idea how creative the teenagers could be in turning harmless items into weapons.

While I was visiting the treatment center in Roslindale, the teenagers were supposed to attend two different rehabilitative groups: one dealing with substance abuse, the other with anger management. Both followed the principles of dialectic behavioral therapy. Several clinicians on staff also met with the teenagers at least once a week. Only during their final months, as the young men were transitioning back into the community, were they allowed to attend school outside the building and spend time in their own family homes.

Three teenagers I interviewed in Boston were placed in a "staff-secure setting." One such treatment center was located close to Plymouth, Massachusetts, in the middle of a nature preserve. The facility was so remote that it could be reached by traveling over narrow dirt roads for half an hour. The treatment center was surrounded by a forest overlooking a picturesque lake. The setting seemed that of a summer camp rather than a DYS facility—an impression amplified by a large totem pole erected in the driveway that the DYS shared with the adjacent Boy Scout camp.

The teenagers lived in several small white houses and seemed able to move relatively freely between the facility's houses. Every time I visited, several teenagers were outside playing basketball. The young men had to wear specified clothing and adhere to the facility's rules, such as set bedtimes, eating schedules, and school attendance.

Another participant in my study was assigned to a similar environment about an hour and a half west of Boston in North Grafton. Yet another of the committed teenagers had to remain in Dorchester and spent four months in a group home, the security level of which seemed to be between the more lenient placements in the countryside and the highly secured prison in Roslindale. All facilities were staffed with clinicians. Rehabilitative programming consisted of groups adhering to the rules of dialectic behavioral therapy. Except for those at the treatment center in Roslindale, the teenagers were taken on field trips.

Juvenile prisons run by the Illinois Department of Juvenile Justice were far less eclectic in their design than DYS treatment centers. Like adult prisons, the facilities were divided into minimum-, medium-, and maximum-security facilities.[13] The state ran seven juvenile prisons across Illinois. Two of the children in the Chicago study were committed to the Illinois Youth Center in St. Charles (IYC–St. Charles) and returned to the prison multiple times over the course of two years. One of them also spent time at the Illinois Youth Center Chicago (IYC-Chicago). I was not able to visit juvenile prisons in Illinois for research purposes, though I worked at IYC-Chicago as a volunteer for a theater group.

IYC-Chicago was a minimum-security prison. Some of the inmates were referred there because they were in danger of violating their parole. Constructed during the mid-1990s, the building was originally intended to house violent offenders. In addition to cognitive behavioral therapy and dialectic behavioral therapy group sessions, IYC-Chicago offered several therapeutic interventions, such as a psychotherapeutic program dealing with trauma and stress in adolescence. Nevertheless, IYC-Chicago continued to operate according to the rules of a prison. The youths had to wear jumpsuits. When I visited the facility, different colors of jumpsuit indicated different levels of privileges. Visitors had to pass through a metal detector. The visiting area resembled visitation rooms in adult prisons, with the obligatory vending machine, bleak tables, and chairs where the inmate and his visitor sat across from each other.

IYC–St. Charles was a medium-security facility that I was never able to visit. The facility had a reputation for being understaffed and overly punitive. One of the biggest concerns of the John Howard Association, a nonprofit organization that regularly visits Illinois juvenile justice institutions, was IYC–St. Charles's excessive reliance on solitary confinement. The association reported that between April 2011 and April 2012 the facility used solitary confinement 792 times for an inmate population that averaged 148 men. The average length a teenager remained in solitary confinement was 2.28 days.

Probation and Parole

After their release from the various juvenile justice institutions, teenagers had to adhere to probation or parole requirements. In Massachusetts the probation officers were part of the Massachusetts Juvenile Court Department and worked independently from the DYS. In Boston, probation requirements ranged from strictly monitored home confinement to a curfew and regular check-ins with the probation officer. Depending on their cases, teenagers in Boston also had to do community service and participate in group therapy or individual counseling. They had to attend and do well in school or were assigned to programs designed to transition them into employment.

If a teenager repeatedly did not comply with the conditions of his probation, he was sent to a detention facility. If he was arrested for a new crime, he was likely committed to one of the DYS treatment centers. After a young man had been committed to the DYS, the probation officer was no longer responsible for the case and a DYS caseworker took over.

A caseworker was supposed to visit the teenager while he was in treatment. These visits became more regular as the release date drew closer. Once a teenager was released, his caseworker became the central figure in his reentry process. The caseworker determined the teenager's postincarceration treatment and supervision with the help of a standard actuarial assessment tool. Caseworkers also drew on so-called educational, clinical, and family specialists who could be integrated into the teenagers' treatment plan as the caseworkers saw fit.

Probation regulations, as well as parole requirements, were more rigorously enforced for the Boston teenagers. Failing to call in and missing appointments were always noted, and consequences followed swiftly. The requirements for paroled teenagers were more extensive and all-encompassing than for the teenagers on probation, but both groups told me that they hardly found the time to participate in activities (e.g., attending a little sister's birthday party or engaging in sports) that were not organized by the DYS or the probation department.

Probation requirements in Chicago also included community service, regular school attendance, and several interventions that had been introduced within the framework of JDAI in the mid-1990s. Evening Reporting Centers, for example, were established in 1995 to provide teenagers otherwise confined to the JTDC with an after-school program that seemed to consist of playing games and hanging out with other teenagers on probation.

The fifteen Cook County children interacted only sporadically with their probation officers and had hardly any mental health support. Their program assignments were sometimes arbitrary. One teenager who ended up in juvenile prison could have avoided incarceration if he had submitted to a substance abuse program. Aside from smoking marijuana occasionally, he was not struggling with addiction, and he therefore refused to go to drug rehabilitation center. His probation officer realized that the teenager did not have a drug problem, but he still believed that "being in rehab is better than being sent to DOC [the Department of Corrections]."

Teenagers regularly violated their probation requirements, but because probation officers did not always keep appointments or report violations, some teenagers were able to push the boundaries of their sentences.

Once a teenager was released from an Illinois juvenile prison, he could be placed on juvenile parole. The system of juvenile parole in Chicago has been criticized by the Illinois Juvenile Justice Commission, an advisory committee to the governor, as following an "adult surveillance model." The commission particularly noted that juvenile parolees were supervised by the parole officers of the Department of Corrections and were monitored according to adult standards. The commission further criticized the lack of a case management system that would allow parole officers to develop a more integrated form of aftercare.[14] The two Chicago teenagers who had to spend time in a juvenile prison continued to be on probation for other cases after they had been released. Their interaction with the juvenile justice system therefore continued to be framed by their probation requirements.

CONCLUSION: BRIDGING REHABILITATION AND PUNISHMENT

I spent almost four years researching the juvenile justice systems of Boston and Chicago. During this time I repeatedly witnessed how the contradictory institutional logic of punishment and rehabilitation defeated the individual efforts of staff members, probation officers, teachers, and social workers to help struggling youths.

Almost everybody I met who was connected to the juvenile justice system tried to improve the lives of the teenagers who participated in my research. Yet social workers, probation officers, and juvenile judges were constrained by a bureaucracy designed to administer to struggling youths efficiently and, more imperatively, cost-effectively. Juvenile justice as an institution fundamentally lacked the ability to make fine distinctions between cases or to provide individualized support (Weber 1979). As the following chapters elaborate in greater detail, teenagers and juvenile justice workers alike compensated for a slow and grueling bureaucratic process by drawing on the narrative of the "American Dream." From the perspective of a social worker, upholding the idea of the United States as a meritocratic society eased the burden of not being able to do enough for a client.

Appealing to the teenagers' agency, even though the odds were stacked against them, also conveniently bridged rehabilitative and punitive aspects of juvenile justice. The belief that American society would open up for young minority men if they changed their ways and worked hard enough framed punitive experiences in a rehabilitative light. Detention could be understood as an opportunity to learn from mistakes; incarceration was a time of reflection and self-scrutiny after which a new person was supposed to emerge.

The experiences of the teenagers in Boston and Chicago overlapped in significant ways. Chapters 3, 4, and 5 emphasize the similarities in the teenagers' experience. Despite astonishing similarities between both systems, the different level of resources available to them generated different trajectories of desistance and recidivism. Chapter 6 demonstrates how different ways of executing juvenile justice shaped those trajectories. Finally, the different bureaucratic structures in Boston and Chicago also influenced the kind of data I was able to collect in each city. The appendix provides an in-depth discussion of this methodological challenge.

3 Too Little Too Late

JUVENILE JUSTICE AS A SOCIAL SERVICE PROVIDER

I met Demetrius at the Healy North Alternative School in July 2010, when he was fifteen years old. He was on probation for armed robbery and had violated his home confinement. Rather than being held at the JTDC, he was sent to the Saura Center. Over the course of the two years I met with Demetrius, he was held once at the Saura Center and three times at the JTDC. Twice he was committed to St. Charles, a juvenile prison outside Chicago. During the summer of 2011, Demetrius was shot seven times in the legs. He was released from the hospital after nine days, but he did not take his antibiotics as prescribed. As a result, his wounds became infected again, the antibiotics stopped working, and he spent most of fall 2011 and winter 2012 in a hospital bed. During spring 2012, Demetrius seemed to be getting better—he walked around on crutches and his health was clearly improving. Unable to move for almost a year, Demetrius had succeeded in staying out of trouble.

From the perspective of the juvenile justice system, Demetrius had finally turned a corner: a teenager who, according to his public defender, had a staggering nineteen cases on his criminal record had not been involved in any crime for a whole year. Demetrius's pending cases were dismissed and he was released from juvenile probation. No more curfews, urine tests, ankle bracelets, or community service. In May 2012, for the first time in years, Demetrius was completely free of any obligation to the Chicago juvenile justice system. His freedom didn't last long. Half a year later Demetrius was arrested again for armed robbery. Now seventeen, he was sent to Cook County Jail. As of March 2016, more than three years later, he remained incarcerated there.

Demetrius lived in a poor neighborhood on Chicago's South Side that was heavily patrolled by the Chicago police. He and his older brother were known in the neighborhood for causing trouble. When Demetrius proudly told me that he was off probation, I was pessimistic about his ability to stay away from the streets; and I was not surprised when I heard that he had been arrested again. Demetrius life course could easily be understood solely as an outcome of racial profiling, constant surveillance, and mass incarceration of African American men (A. Goffman 2014; Western 2006). Without a doubt, Demetrius had experienced his share of police harassment and racial profiling. Nevertheless, he was not simply a product of the "youth control complex"—a juvenile justice system that punishes young minority men and infiltrates even neutral social institutions, such as families and schools (Rios 2011, 40–41).

Even if Demetrius had never been arrested again, he would not have achieved his middle-class dreams of having a well-paying job and taking care of his many siblings. At seventeen he was illiterate. He had no stable home to come back to. His family was poor and had been poor for generations. Demetrius had to raise himself. His main problem was not an overbearing juvenile justice system. It was the utter lack of any social service that he could access independently from being on probation or parole. Paradoxically, being off probation made his situation worse and left him without any of the—albeit meager—rehabilitative support mechanisms that juvenile justice continued to provide in Chicago despite its bad reputation.

When I talked to Demetrius for the first time, we realized we had acquaintances in common through the Precious Blood Center in Englewood, where I had begun my fieldwork in 2009. Demetrius was very likeable, a skinny, athletic fifteen-year-old with long dreadlocks and a broad smile. He was a "bucket boy": together with his brother he belonged to a group of young men who played buckets as drums in front of the Art

Institute, Wrigley Field, or the White Sox stadium. Demetrius was eager to enroll in my study when I recruited him. As I did with the other teenagers, I asked him to write down his mother's name, address, and phone number. He explained that his handwriting looked weird because his hand had been smashed in a door. Demetrius wrote down his first and last name in block letters. He told me his mother's phone number, and I prompted him to spell his mother's first name. He smiled self-consciously, stumbled with a few letters, but then admitted that he was not sure how to spell it. I quickly realized he could not write anything but his own name and could not read either. In December 2011, I visited him at La Rabida Children's Hospital in Chicago, where he was treated for his gunshot wounds. He was supposed to choose what he wanted to eat from a menu sitting on his side table. He handed the menu to me and asked me to read the options to him and check off the choices he made.

It was also obvious that Demetrius struggled with being in a regular classroom. He could not sit still. During one of the group sessions I observed, he lay down and began to roll around on the floor. He said his back hurt and he could not sit on a chair. Other teenagers in the room began to make fun of him, and it was almost impossible to continue with the group session. Demetrius was supposed to enroll in school after he was released from the Saura Center in August 2010, but he never did. His mother told me, "He hasn't been in school at all. He refuses to go; I don't know what his problem is." Demetrius told me that he does not want to go to school, because there is just "too much fighting. . . . I don't like the kids who go there." Another teenager who was enrolled in my study and attended Healy North described how excruciating it must have been for Demetrius to attend school with other teenagers. "He [Demetrius] tried to read one day. I thought he was playing around and I started laughing and then I just stopped for a second . . . he was like, 'Doo da doo.' I was like, 'Damn, you are retarded.' He couldn't read." Despite his illiteracy, Demetrius had passed eighth grade.

Demetrius came from an extremely unstable home. His mother had seven children, the youngest of whom was two years old when I began interviewing Demetrius. According to Demetrius the relationship between his mother and her boyfriend was volatile and involved physical abuse. The one time I met his mother's boyfriend, he seemed to be under the influence of drugs or alcohol. His pupils were the size of pinheads. His speech was slurred. In addition to his mother, six siblings, and stepfather, Demetrius's uncle also lived with the family. On my last visit in May 2012 Demetrius told me that his uncle's mental health was deteriorating:

> [He is] going crazy . . . he be getting high, breaking holes through our wall. I try to calm him down, get him to eat something. They gotta send him back to rehab so that they can give him his medicine. He is not taking it. Because if he be taking his medicine, he be calm. But I think that is not want he wants to do. He wants to be running around laughing, being funny.

Understandably, Demetrius was rarely home, even at times when he was not in detention, prison, or the hospital. Although he was enthusiastic about enrolling in my study, Demetrius had a difficult time showing up to the appointments we made. Several times I arrived at his house and his mother told me that he had just left. She said he came home only to sleep, if at all.

As long as Demetrius was held in the various juvenile justice facilities, and while he was outside on probation, the benefits were minimal but still existent. At least he attended school at the Saura Center. While nobody taught him how to read, the principal spent extra time to teach him math. He was forced to keep a regular schedule, and there were adults in his life who were providing food, shelter, and occasional emotional support. For Demetrius the juvenile justice system was not just a controlling force; it was the only social support network he had.

Demetrius's case was not an anomaly. Juvenile justice workers were often the only people providing a modicum of help, such as clothing vouchers, therapy, food, or after-school programs, to struggling inner-city teenagers and their families. The juvenile justice systems in Boston and Chicago continued to fulfill their original welfare function—even if they did so inefficiently.

The inefficiencies of the systems were closely related to their dual function as punitive and rehabilitative agencies (Platt 1977; Zimring 2005). Rehabilitative social services, for instance, were usually reserved for those teenagers who had already committed severe crimes or multiple offenses: "high-risk" youths. First-time offenders, petty thieves, status offenders, or teenagers who, like Demetrius, had officially desisted from crime were excluded not only from the punitive but also from the social welfare aspects of juvenile justice. Even in cases where the child protection side of the system came into effect, the social services the young men received were narrowly designed to address their criminal behavior. After all, parents had often relinquished custody because they did not want to deal with their children's criminality anymore. Assigning youths to the juvenile justice system was in many cases a better option than leaving struggling teenagers to fend for themselves. Yet the juvenile justice system in both cities was not equipped to deal with the familial or mental health problems that co-occurred with the teenagers' criminal behavior.

Jamal's probation officer, for example, initially struggled to find services for his client, simply because he was arrested for only minor crimes. Jamal was fifteen years old when he signed up to participate in my study in July 2010. He was small for his age and looked like a child in comparison to his classmates. He had big black eyes and short hair. Jamal's enthusiasm and respectful demeanor made him very likeable. He was eager to participate in the group sessions Scholarship and Guidance Association (SGA) ran at Healy North, and he was also very vocal about his desire to change his life.[1] His goals were straightforward: "Finish school, get a job, have my own family one day." Jamal's crimes were comparatively harmless misdemeanors. It was his domestic situation that caused his continuous involvement with the Chicago juvenile justice system.

Jamal lived with his grandparents and two half-siblings on Chicago's far South Side. The neighborhood was almost suburban, with neatly mowed lawns and carefully decorated front porches. Jamal's home was one of the more run-down buildings in the area. The exterior paint was peeling. Inside, the house was stuffy and cluttered. Half-filled boxes stood in the hallway, piles of clothes covered the furniture, and dog hair was everywhere. His grandmother, who had recently undergone chemotherapy for breast cancer, was exhausted and overwhelmed by the housework and by the responsibility of taking care of three children when she herself was ill and in her sixties.

When she and I talked about Jamal during the summer of 2010, she told me, "I can't do it anymore. I am tired. I am sick. I need to take care of myself." She also said that before her illness she had gone to school regularly to check on Jamal and see if he had been keeping up with his work, but of late she had been unable to do so. In her opinion, this was when Jamal's behavior worsened. She and her husband had adopted Jamal and his half-siblings about a decade before when their mother officially abandoned all three children. Jamal had never lived with his mother, and he struggled with not knowing her at all. He and his two siblings did not share the same father. Jamal claimed that his grandparents treated him differently from his half-siblings. His grandparents were the parents of his siblings' father, so he was not directly related to them. His grandmother vehemently denied Jamal's accusation.

Shortly after Jamal enrolled in the study, it was already unclear if he would be able to return home after his release from the Saura Center. His grandmother refused to let him back into her house. Jamal claimed he knew a family that would be willing to take him in. His probation officer contacted them to ask if they were going to take custody of Jamal. He told me that Jamal had actually lived with them for a few months before he came to the Saura Center but that they had no desire to let him move back in. "Stuff in the house went missing, and he went around the neighborhood telling people that they were not giving him any food." Jamal's probation officer eventually convinced his grandmother to allow her grandson back into the house, and he returned home in August 2010.

Initially Jamal was happy about being back: "It's better than being locked up." Unfortunately, his home life deteriorated quickly after his return. He began to accuse his grandparents of neglecting him and also claimed that his uncle was abusive. Jamal said that he did not own any clothes, not even underwear. Jamal's probation officer recalled what happened on a visit to the grandparents' house at the end of August: "I came by the house to check on him. He had claimed that he has nothing to wear. We were on the porch and his aunt brought down Jamal's clothes. We went through every piece and identified it as Jamal's. He then claimed that he doesn't have any underwear. So his aunt goes up again and brought down his underwear. He broke down crying and said that everyone is against him."

Meanwhile his probation officer told me that he suspected Jamal struggled with a severe mental illness. He seemed to have a perception of reality completely different from that of the adults around him. At a minimum, the officer thought Jamal was a compulsive liar. Although he tried to get him mental health support, the probation officer had no luck finding an adequate intervention. All the programs had already filled up, and because his adoption had been finalized a long time ago, his family was not eligible for any postadoption services. Around the same time, I also received a glimpse into the tensions that prevailed in Jamal's home. On arriving at the house on a Sunday morning in late August, I recorded the following scene in my field notes:

> As I drive up to the house, I can see that there is a red car parked in front of it. The side windows are smashed. Jamal is cleaning up the glass that is spattered on the ground. His uncle is agitated, walking up and down the entryway. When I get out of my car and walk towards the house, he yells at me: "Take him with you! I am sick of this! These kids have gotten me into trouble too many times.[2] It is not my job to fix them! Take him with you!" He suspects that Jamal and his friend are responsible for smashing up his car windows: "A few days ago he [Jamal] told me that he was going to break into my car when he was mad at me and now look at this. It was him!" Jamal claims that he had nothing to do with it. We all go into the house and I try to talk to Jamal about what happened. Jamal sits on the living room sofa. He stares into space and does not want to talk at all. After a while he just gets up and leaves. After about 5 more minutes I am leaving the house as well. I see him hanging out on his neighbor's front porch, talking to a couple of his friends.

By the end of September 2010 Jamal had to wear an ankle bracelet and was on home confinement, having been found guilty for an old burglary case. In the meantime his sister had been admitted to a psychiatric ward. He was very frustrated with his living situation. "I should have stayed where I was [the Saura Center]. I want to get off home confinement so I don't have to be in the house." Jamal also emphasized that he really wanted to change. "The only thing I am trying to focus on right now is my school." Yet he said that his grandmother just kept yelling at him for no reason. He suspected that "she just wants me to get locked up again." By November 2010 Jamal was indeed again at the JTDC, because he had missed his curfew and did not appear in court. For the next few months he went back and forth between his grandmother's house and the juvenile detention center because he did not keep up with probation requirements. He was missing school, failing his classes, getting into fights, and barely showing up at home.

In spring 2011 his grandparents finally decided that they would not take him back. In April, during one of Jamal's court cases, I was introduced to his mentor, Darryl,[3] who offered a very grim view of Jamal's situation. "Jamal is actually lying about a lot of stuff, and he does not comply with what is asked from him. We [the social work agency he worked for] offered Jamal a job. He would have just had to come to the office, be there to do some homework, and clean the place up a bit, but he wouldn't do it."

At the same time, Darryl believed that the whole family was lying about everything that went on in the house. He said, "Jamal has just learned that lying is the way to handle life, and there is no doubt that Jamal is neglected by his grandparents." Darryl was also convinced that Jamal received occasional beatings by his uncle. During the court date when I met Darryl, the judge decided to transfer custody from his grandparents to the state. Jamal had to remain at the JTDC for another few weeks before being transferred to a temporary group home. He did not want to go there. He told me that he wanted to have a real family.

Jamal was lucky that, after another few weeks passed, his DCFS caseworker seemed to have found a foster mother for him. In a brief conversation with his caseworker, I realized that she had no knowledge of Jamal's struggles or his compulsive lying. She told me that Jamal was going to spend some time with his new foster mother on the upcoming weekend. According to Jamal's caseworker, the foster mother was open-minded about the fact that teenagers make mistakes sometimes. She requested only one thing: honesty. In October 2011, I had another conversation with Jamal's caseworker, in which she expressed what she saw as effort wasted on Jamal:

> I sacrificed my own time for him. . . . I had found a very nice family for him. He was supposed to go over there, spend the weekend with them. . . . Her kids are all grown up and she was willing to provide a good home for him. But he never showed up for the meeting. He said that he couldn't go because the house he was at during the time would not give him his check [the implication is that he did not have any money to buy a bus or train ticket]. I called the shelter and they said that this is not true. He ran away on the day he was supposed to be at this new family's house. He did not come home all night. And as he started lying, I thought to myself: I am not gonna do that to this nice family. This is a foster family that you wish for. I am not gonna

place him with this poor woman. I think he is not fit to be placed with a foster family at all. . . . He called me again and wanted something, but I told him, "I am through with you; you played me well."

When I asked her if Jamal ever had a mental health evaluation, she said no but that it was probably going to happen once he had been placed at a group home permanently.

At this point, Jamal had been involved with the juvenile justice system in Chicago for almost two years. During the time I followed him through the system, no one but his probation officer ever mentioned the possibility that Jamal's struggles could be related to mental illness,[4] even though his sister had a documented history of severe mental problems. It was clear to me that Jamal was struggling with extreme mood swings. He could be a very respectful, friendly, and talkative teenager who would sometimes welcome me with a brief hug and a smile. Then a week later he could be cold, barely making eye contact with me and interested only in the money he received for meeting with me. At the DCFS, nobody was aware of his family background or his struggles with compulsive lying. As a result, his caseworker, who was there to support him, withdrew because she felt used. By the end of November 2011, Jamal refused to cooperate with anyone. He insulted the staff members at the group home that was supposed to be his final placement. As one of the staff members recalled, he repeated one sentence over and over again: "I am almost finna be seventeen years old. No one can tell me what to do."

It was quite obvious that Jamal and his family were in desperate need of social services, mental health support, and a social worker who could help the ailing grandmother to parent her teenage grandchildren effectively. The support the family did receive was accessible only through Jamal's involvement with juvenile justice; and the juvenile justice system was a blunt tool for addressing an extremely delicate and complex familial situation.

By the time Jamal was officially transferred to the child protection side of the Chicago juvenile justice system, miscommunication and lack of information made it extremely difficult to intervene in meaningful ways. His run-ins with the law overshadowed other pathologies, such as his compulsive lying. His untreated mental health problems served to alienate those people who were supposed to help him. Jamal entered a downward spiral in which he distrusted everyone and began to play the part of the bad boy more and more convincingly. Eventually he was placed in a long-term group home about an hour northwest of Chicago. He stayed there for a week, but when he was not allowed to go to Chicago to attend a home-coming ball, he packed his suitcase. Before he left, it was said, he told the other teenagers in the house that "he was going to go home soon anyway." When he resurfaced, he was sent to yet another group home, from which he disappeared in February 2012 for a longer period, prompting the DCFS to file a missing-person report. Jamal remained on the run until July 2012, when the police arrested him for aggravated use of an unlawful weapon. The seventeen-year-old, now considered an adult, was sentenced to a one-year prison term with the Illinois Department of Corrections. As of March 2016 he was again incarcerated, this time serving a four-year sentence for residential burglary.

In Boston, the juvenile justice system took over welfare functions for struggling families even more completely than in Chicago. Darell's mother, for example, believed that her son was well cared for when he was in the detention center. She had the impression that that the DYS offered effec-tive programs and remarked that "they do a lot with these kids." In Darell's case the juvenile justice system tried to address underlying familial issues that seemed related to his acting out. Like the other teenagers in Boston, I recruited Darell at the Eliot Detention Center in Dorchester. He joined the study in February 2012, when he was fifteen years old. Darell, his mother, and his younger brother and sister lived in a Section 8 apartment in South Boston. In December 2011 he and his brother had been arrested for an unarmed robbery. He did not have to spent time in the detention center but received probation. By February 2012 he was rearrested for theft. This time he was incarcerated at the Eliot Detention Center for approximately three weeks, before his mother posted bail and he could return home at the beginning of March.

Over the following months he bounced back and forth between the detention center and his home in such quick succession that it was chal-lenging to keep track. Two weeks after he was sent home in March, he was back at the detention center because his mother had revoked her bail. She claimed that he had been trying to break into her room. After a few days in detention, his mother changed her mind and posted bail again, and Darell returned home. Three weeks later he was back at Eliot yet again. According to his mother, he missed his curfew six times and was suspended from school. "This time it wasn't me who got him locked up," she said.

Darell's mother was not ready for him to return home. His charges were not significant enough to warrant commitment to a DYS treatment facility, so his mother filed a CHINS case. As a result, Darell was assigned a DCF caseworker and, by mid-June, transferred to a group home. He was allowed to come home on weekends to spent time with his family. Darell seemed to like it at the shelter at first and claimed that the house was providing him with the structure he needed to stay out of trouble. He mentioned that he, his mother, and the court evaluator had agreed that going to a family therapy program might help him. He also admitted that he just wanted to get out of the detention center and show the judge that he could do well in the community.

As time went on and he was still not allowed to return to his mother's place permanently, Darell became less compliant and more irritated with his living conditions. When I asked Darell about his living situation, his frustration spilled out of him. From his perspective, being at the group home had ceased being useful for him after he had been there for a few months:

> Every single day there is a new rule. . . . If little things happen, they call the police immediately. And they don't think about what it means to be stuck here all day. The program director, who is barely ever there, she is just so uptight. She doesn't understand that being stuck in the house is not good at all. We eat. We just sit on it. That is not good. You are supposed to get some exercise. . . . It's punishment. I am ready [to move back home]. I am just waiting for them to say, "Come home."

After his CHINS case was opened, Darell received family therapy and he was supposed to meet weekly with his clinician at the group home. He perceived the mental health services as helpful at first, yet being held at the group home remained a punitive experience for him.

It was also quite obvious that Darell's mother used the CHINS case as a tool for enforcing discipline. At the end of November 2012 I had just finished my interview with Darell and we were trying to find a time for a meeting during the upcoming week. Darell was allowed to have home passes if his mother agreed that he could come by during the week. He asked his mother, "Mom, do you know when I will be home next week?" His mother snapped back, "Don't be bugging me; we will see how the rest of the weekend goes! You know the rules, don't be getting on my nerves." For Darell's mother the CHINS case had bestowed on her new means of enforcing the behavior she desired in her son. As a result, the therapeutic intervention had turned into a punitive tool that allowed Darell's mother to exercise control over her son.

Even though Darell's mother used juvenile justice interventions to regulate her son's behavior, the entanglement of welfare and punishment did not have an unequivocally negative effect on his life. In Darell's case, the Boston juvenile justice system had provided him and his family with valuable services. If Darell had not been punished, he would have had even less support.

José, on the other hand, was one of the teenagers in Boston who never crossed the threshold for receiving any social services. José was fourteen years old when I met him in the Eliot Detention Center in Dorchester in April 2012. He and his mother emigrated from Colombia to the United States when he was seven years old. His father had left six years earlier to move to the United States. The only language spoken at home was Spanish. José also had a little brother, who was born in the United States and was ten years younger than he. The family lived in a small two-bedroom apartment in East Boston. The offense he was on probation for was relatively harmless—unarmed robbery. Yet, over the course of nine months, José went in and out of the detention center four times because he did not comply with his probation requirements. José was also struggling with his parents. Yet, unlike Darell, José was never turned over to DCF. Since he had officially been involved in only one case, he was considered low risk. The restrictions imposed on him were adhering to a 7:30 P.M. curfew, going to school, and doing thirty hours of community service.

José's familial problems stemmed from growing up in two different cultures. He did not respect his parents, because of their inability to interact effectively with their English-speaking environment. When his enrollment in school was delayed after he was released from the Eliot detention in September 2012, for instance, his parents did not know what to do to get him back in school. They showed me papers they had received and asked me if I understood what was going on. José got upset when his mother approached me, because he had apparently already explained to them that his enrollment process had started but that it took time for the paperwork to make its way through the system. He looked at me and said in English: "See, I told you. That is why it is so hard to live with them. They just don't believe it when I tell them something. They don't understand, but they don't believe me. It's embarrassing!"

José was also upset with his parents because he thought it was their fault that he went back and forth between his home and jail. At the end of October, having just been released from his third stint in the Eliot Detention Center, he told me:

> I think my life is fucked up because of them [his parents]. The only thing she [his mother] had to do is tell the judge, "He is doing his best." She always thinks I want her to lie. I don't want her to lie. I just don't want her to tell the judge that I missed curfew and stuff. Being locked up that doesn't help me. I get madder and madder. . . . They [his parents] think they are helping me, but they are not. The streets are still in there [in the detention center]. It is worse in there. When I am in jail and I have a problem with someone, I have to see that person every day. In the street we beat each other up and leave. In jail I have to see this person and every day I have to think about getting smarter, otherwise he will beat me up.

José was stuck in a destructive cycle. The quick succession of going back and forth between the detention center and the community did nothing but disrupt his already fragile commitment to going to school, confirming his blasé attitude toward the world and strengthening his commitment to crime. By the end of December, José had not been in school regularly for a whole year. It always took several weeks to reenroll him in school after he was released, and just when he started to go to school again, he would violate his probation requirements and be sent back to the Eliot Detention Center.

Realizing the absurdity of the situation, José believed the juvenile justice system had turned into a disciplining tool for his parents. "I think my mom uses court to her advantage, to make me do what she wants me to do." His parents indeed grasped at straws when they continued to report their son's probation violations. His father told me that they had tried to ask people at José's school for help but nobody could help them. His parents suspected there was more going on than just his coming home late, and they were extremely worried about José. They were desperate to get someone to pay attention to him. When I met his father for the first time, he explained to me: "José doesn't want to go to school. He doesn't listen. We don't know what to do." Then he offered me money to talk to his son. "We will pay anything; we have to pay," he said. I had to explain to him that I am not a therapist and that I was meeting with their son only to do research.

If José had been arrested for a more severe crime, the juvenile justice system in Boston would likely have expended more rehabilitative resources on him, for example, by helping him find a job or enrolling him in therapeutic services. Yet, because José was never caught for any serious crime, longer-term interventions were deemed unnecessary. In the end, rather than challenging his destructive worldview, his continuous exposure to the juvenile justice system seemed only to strengthen his deviant identity.

José's trajectory demonstrates vividly that castigating juvenile justice as overly punitive is too simplistic. In poor neighborhoods with few, if any, after-school programs or jobs available, being punished by the juvenile justice system may provide access to these scarce goods. Absurdly, the easiest way for a teenager to become eligible for social services in Boston or Chicago was to get arrested for armed robbery.

A PARADOX REVISITED

The two juvenile justice systems I studied continued to struggle with their hybrid institutional structure. Juvenile justice in Boston and Chicago attempted to address poverty, family dysfunction, violence, and lack of education. Often their interventions came too late—after drug addictions had already manifested; after abuse had taken place; after schools had given up and innocent people had been hurt.

The dynamics of social service provision and punishment in Boston and Chicago overlapped but also differed in important ways. In Chicago, rehabilitative measures were not streamlined and seemed to depend largely on the effort a probation officer put forward on behalf of his or her client (Jacobs 1993). As Jamal's example shows, because individuals were positively disposed toward him, he had access to a mentor and was almost placed with a foster family. Such individual efforts are fragile without an official structure that fosters exchange of information between the different administrative branches (Jacobs 1993). No official mental health evaluation, or even communication between the probation officer and the DCFS caseworker, occurred that could have alerted the DCFS to a potential mental health issue.

Rehabilitative measures were more readily available in Boston and better coordinated than in Chicago. Yet those social services were also related primarily to the young men's deviant behavior. The juvenile justice system in Boston seemed a coercive tool for parents that allowed them to exert pressure on their teenage children. Because eligibility for social services was so closely tied to deviance, teenagers who had not been caught with severe enough crimes, or whose parents did not file a CHINS case, had difficulty getting access to any support mechanisms—therapy, for example. In José's case, exposure to the juvenile justice system offered no service that could have addressed his identity struggles. Being in the system, rather, interrupted his education and set him back further.

CONCLUSION: THE CHOICE OF HAPPINESS

In one of our interviews José and I talked about happiness and what it takes to be happy. For him happiness was connected to having money: "Rich people have a choice not to be happy. Poor people don't have a choice." From his perspective rich people created their problems artificially. There was nothing that couldn't be solved with money. This simplistic view reflected his social position. His family was poor. His parents worked at multiple restaurants and barely managed to make ends meet. He asked me, "Why is it a crime to be hustling?" He believed that poor people were just trying to make a living. "They have nothing and they don't know anything else."

José came from an immigrant family whose hope for a better life disintegrated further as their son struggled to find his place in US society. It is easy to sympathize with José's parents. They left Colombia, a country embroiled in a drug war, to find peace and security in the United States. They worked hard and did their best with the limited means they had. It is much harder to understand the choices Jamal's, Demetrius's and Darell's families made. Why did women stay with abusive partners? Why did men not manage hold down a well-paying job? When we start blaming the teenagers' families, though, we forget that disadvantage, just like privilege, is inherited, reproduced, and strengthened over generations (Bourdieu 1984; Lareau 2003; Khan 2011).

The juvenile justice system is one of the only institutions left that tries to address the decades of discrimination, racism, poverty, and violence that have shaped families like those described in this chapter. Juvenile justice may not be a suitable candidate for filling the vacancy that the 1990s welfare reform has created (Wacquant 2008). Yet, as far as social services go, having a caring probation officer was often as good as the help was going to get for the teenagers I interviewed. Focusing only on the hypercriminalization of young minority men distracts from the teenagers' struggles, which go well beyond their interactions with police and juvenile judges. Even without police harassment, drug tests, curfews, and ankle bracelets, Demetrius, Jamal, Darell, and José lived deprived and limited lives. José's home was just a fifteen-minute drive from downtown Boston. What were his chances of ever working in one of the high-rise buildings as anything other than a doorman? How likely was Demetrius to find a job that would offer him a living wage—without being able to read?

Taking the dreams and hopes of young inner-city men seriously does not necessarily culminate in demanding a less punitive juvenile justice system. Rather, it implies stopping the use of juvenile justice as a social welfare provider and, consequently, conceptualizing social services not as a privilege that needs to be controlled, but as a responsibility of the community to the individual. To put it in José's words: Happiness should become choice for poor people as well.

4 Imagining Desistance

I always felt uncomfortable when staff members escorted me out of treatment centers or detention facilities after my interviews in Boston. Around the holidays—Thanksgiving, Christmas, and New Year's—I felt even worse that I could go back to my suburban bubble, while the teenagers I interviewed had to spend the holidays away from their families. Most juvenile justice facilities I visited in Massachusetts did try to make the holidays more bearable for the young men. They served a turkey dinner on Thanksgiving, and in some treatment centers teenagers even received gifts for Christmas. Still, in my view such treats were small consolation for having to spend the holidays in juvenile justice detention.

While I dwelled on my privilege as a researcher, the teenagers kept up a front during the holiday season. They wanted to focus on the positive: what they had learned while they were inside, and how far they had come since their admission. The difference between my perception and the teenagers' desire to make the best out of a bad situation was indicative of their attitude toward being incarcerated year-round. The teenagers usually blamed themselves for their current situation and believed the onus was on them to do better after their release.

In a moment when the young men were unable to make any choices of their own, they focused on their agency. Separated from their usual distractions, teenagers had a lot of time to reflect on their mistakes and to plan for their future. Everybody I interviewed—regardless of whether they were held at a group home in Chicago or the most secure treatment center in Boston—believed that being incarcerated had changed them and that they would never return to any juvenile justice facility again. The teenagers framed their incarceration as a learning experience, a turning point that would allow them to start a new life (Sampson and Laub 2005).

The young men's belief in the deterrent effect of their incarceration stood in stark contrast to their later experience of recidivism and personal failure. Eleven out the fifteen teenagers in Chicago returned to prison or jail at least once over the course of this study. Seven of the young men were held in Cook County Jail for crimes they had committed after their seventeenth birthdays. In Boston two of the teenagers spent most of the observational period in a juvenile prison. One of them was rearrested less than a month after coming home. Of the remaining six youths, five recidivated at least once. They either had to return to the juvenile detention center in Dorchester or were sent back to a long-term treatment facility. By June 2013, one teenager in Boston and two teenagers in Chicago had successfully completed their juvenile probation. The other respondents remained on adult or juvenile probation or parole, or both.

Irrespective of their later failure to "go straight," the young men had previously developed distinctive ideas about what kind of people they would like to become and how they could implement their transformation. During their pretrial detention or posttrial imprisonment, the idea of "doing the right thing," of "doing what you are told," motivated by the desire to "never be locked up again," was in one form or another expressed by every teenager I interviewed. Yet, aside from the vague notion that they just "had to try hard," the teenagers did not seem to know how they could successfully build a life without crime.

It seems odd that teenagers who have grown up amid racism, poverty, and violence so strongly believed in their agency. Their unrealistic expectations begin to make sense, however, when we look at the conditions of their incarceration. While the youths were held in juvenile justice facilities, they were removed from their accustomed social environment.

Although they were housed with other juvenile offenders, social workers or staff members emphasized the necessity and desirability of self-transformation (Leverentz 2014; Haney 2010). The teenagers began to see themselves through the eyes of the adults who surrounded them (Mead 1969). Furthermore, being locked up in a highly structured environment that enforced new routines encouraged them to perceive their imprisonment as a life-changing event, a turning point (Laub and Sampson 2003).

DOING THE RIGHT THING

Darrius, one of the Chicago teenagers, not only blamed himself but also thought that black youths in general should be held responsible for the violence in Chicago's disadvantaged neighborhoods. When we talked about his experiences in the Chicago public school system, he wondered whether there was something about being African American that predisposed black teenagers to fight with one another. He therefore wanted to attend a school where the majority of students were white.

Darrius had grown up in the Cabrini Green projects. Now his family lived in a mixed-income housing unit that had replaced the infamous public housing projects. He did not like to talk about the details of his childhood, but he admitted that he used marijuana to forget about his experiences growing up in a high-crime area. He explained: "People have been through things in their life, like crazy stuff, you understand? They have seen stuff. Most of the time, well for me, smoking just keeps stuff off my mind. I be focused on what I wanna do. I don't have time on days off to think about that stuff. I try to enjoy myself and that's what I am doing, I enjoy myself."

According to his own recollection, he started committing crimes when he was eleven. He and his friends broke into cabs and stole the drivers' money. Having money and being able to spend it on whatever he wanted drove Darrius to continue robbing people.[1] When I asked him what he did with the money, he said that he would just go out to eat, sometimes to Hooters. "I was just used to having a lot of money for supporting myself. Like if I wanna go buy clothes, I can buy clothes; if I wanna go buy shoes, I can buy shoes, just like every day." For Darrius robbing people was habit.

"I was doing it for so long, without getting caught. It became a sport or something. . . . Whenever I would run out of money, you know, I'd hit another sting."

Although he acknowledged that not having money in his pocket would be challenging, Darrius was very optimistic that he would never have to return to any juvenile justice facility. He believed that the unpleasant experience of being locked up had shown him that is not worth it to commit crimes:

> I be getting tired of going to the Audy Home [the juvenile detention center].
> It is boring in there. I mean, not that it is supposed to be fun, but it's stupid.
> That ain't the place you wanna be. And then at nighttime, they got this
> intercom. In some sections, if you are cool with the staff, they'd be playing
> songs on the intercom so you can hear the songs and stuff, and then you
> think about how you'd be messing with your family. And then a month feel
> like a year, you know. 'Cause the day be getting by so slow. So I just ain't got
> time for that. It's stupid.

He was convinced that he would never be in custody again. "I am done with this [robbing people]. It is all bogus, gangbanging and stuff. I am really not planning on doing it [again]. . . . When I get out of here, I am gonna stay out of trouble, you know, just complete my probation, get my juvenile record expunged and start over from there."

Darrius indeed did well in the Saura Center. He obeyed the rules, and after thirty days his judge allowed him to return home. Yet during the following two years, Darrius returned to the JTDC several times and was sent to juvenile prison three times. In September 2010, he was held at the JTDC because he had violated his curfew and committed another robbery. As a result, he was sent to the juvenile prison in St. Charles for three months, but ended up spending six months. His time was doubled because he fought with another inmate. When he was released in March 2011, I asked him what he had learned and how the six-month confinement had changed him. He replied, "I really don't know, it's just a place where I did not even wanna be." Again he told me that being locked up was so boring that he just did not want to risk going back there again.

Darrius had grown up under extremely difficult circumstances and had a long history of criminal activity. When he was released in March 2011, he returned to his mother's home and his old friends. Darrius needed a thorough reentry plan. Instead he believed that he could almost magically seal himself off from his old environment and his old self.

For a while his strategy of focusing on school and staying away from his friends seemed to work. Yet in July 2011 he was back at the JTDC because he had failed to participate in the outpatient drug rehab program he was supposed to attend. Eventually he was sent to IYC-Chicago, where he had to remain for four months. When I interviewed him after his release, he admitted that he was stuck in a vicious cycle. "It [being in prison] don't help me. Like you be in there thinking, 'When I get out I'll do the right thing,' but once you get out, it's just stuff that you didn't do that you wanted to do 'cause you was locked up. You just try to live life." After not having met with Darrius for almost six months, I called his mother again in May 2012 to set up a final interview. She told me Darrius was again locked up in St. Charles. He was supposed to spend six months there because he had not complied with his probation requirements.

Although Darrius lived most of his early childhood in a violent and impoverished community, not once did he talk to me about his current social position in relation to his upbringing. He did not see himself as a victim of circumstance but wanted to take full responsibility for his actions. Being incarcerated, however, did not offer him any tools that could have given him a chance to leave his past behind. Being locked up had fostered an unrealistic expectation that he could become a different person purely through self-discipline.

Other teenagers understood that going back to their old neighborhood would be challenging. Kendrick, for example, wanted to leave Chicago behind. Shortly after he was admitted to the Saura Center, he already had a plan for his future:

> I'm going to Job Corps,[2] get my GED, because I got kicked out of school. I'm gonna find me a trade in Job Corps and when I found that trade, I am gonna use that trade to the fullest. I'm gonna save my money and if I'm gonna save up a lot of money. I'm gonna end up moving to Texas. I'm gonna end up moving out of state. . . . I just wanna move somewhere I have never been. And Texas, I have never been to Texas. . . . I have never been there, so I wanna try something new. . . . You feel me, if I'm gonna be in Texas, I will be in a whole new environment. I don't know nobody. Nobody know me; I don't know them. I start all over from the beginning.

Kendrick's plan to move out of state was unrealistic. At the time of his arrest he was living with his brother, a college graduate who worked in a call center. Kendrick had stayed with multiple relatives before he had moved in with his brother. He wanted to go to Texas because his brother was supposed to take a job there. His brother, on the other hand, had no desire to share an apartment with Kendrick again. While Kendrick lived with him, he had been an irresponsible roommate. He smoked marijuana, missed school, did not clean up after himself, and hardly came home when he was supposed to. To make matters worse, he also stole from his brother and his brother's other roommate. Kendrick's brother had had enough and was in the process of transferring custody of Kendrick to DCFS. He was not planning on taking Kendrick to Texas with him.

Kendrick also admitted that he was a gang member. He said he joined because he was fascinated by his gang-member friends' lifestyle:

> I always liked how they carried themselves. They had money in their pocket. You asked them where do you get the money from, and they be like, "Well, we work." And I know they not working no real job. So I was like, "I wish that would be me." They had me like, I always saw them with money; I always saw them with the fresh pair of shoes, fresh pair of jeans. They be fresh. And one day, there was this boy I was hanging around, and I called him my brother, 'cause I looked up to him. He gave me money when I needed it. . . . He was like, "You should come home." I was like, "I don't know what you mean?" And he wanted me to join the gang. You feel me, I was young and naive; I wanted to join the gang right along with him. And I joined it.

He started selling marijuana but never got caught. He was eventually arrested for robbery. Initially Kendrick did not have to spend time at the JTDC, but instead was allowed to go home on probation. Asked why he stole from other people, he replied, "I have no idea. It was just like a game. I never really intend to hurt anybody. I was just trying to have fun."

In May 2012 he was arrested again for violation of his probation. His judge decided to send him to the Saura Center. Kendrick's mother had not been in his life since he was a small child, and he had seen his father for the last time when he was eleven. Kendrick was supposed to stay at the Saura Center until the court managed to find a foster home for him, but he remained there only for a few days. He got into fights and was also suspended from school for calling the person who served lunch "Kermit the Frog." After his judge went through the list of infringements, she decided to keep him for several weeks at the JTDC. Kendrick was greatly disappointed, but he also insisted that the second time at the JTDC was really going to change him. "The first time was just a week and some of my friends were there too. Now I am alone and I really feel what it means to be locked up."

Kendrick was clearly fascinated by the gang lifestyle. He was not interested in attending school. The Job Corps placement he talked about proved difficult to get. Aside from the fact that his brother had no intention of taking Kendrick with him, being on juvenile probation would have prevented him from leaving Illinois anyway. Just like Darrius, Kendrick's notion of self-transformation was outcome-oriented and relied on the unrealistic perception that he could reinvent himself if he just tried hard enough.

Shortly after his release from the Saura Center, Ben also blamed himself for his past and was convinced that he would never return to a detention facility again: "I learned my lesson by getting locked up. I have seen [that] the stuff I have been doing was actually stupid." He added, "When you are doing this stuff [committing a crime], you don't actually think about it until something bad happened to you and that's when you decide to, you know, to change around." For almost a year Ben seemed to hold to his commitment to stay away from the streets. Then, in October 2011, he was arrested for breaking and entering. Since the crime took place after his seventeenth birthday, he was sent to Cook County Jail.

The teenagers assumed that they could shed their former self almost effortlessly. Remembering the restrictions of being locked up was supposed to serve as an incentive for exercising extraordinary discipline and "doing the right thing" in the future. The motivation was to turn incarceration into a meaningful event—a turning point after which a better future could be imagined. Yet, during their time away from their neighborhoods, they developed no strategy that would allow them to put this initial cognitive shift into practice. The agency they exercised while they were held in juvenile justice facilities was expressed in the form of submission to institutional rules. Rather than providing the teenagers an opportunity to experience a nondeviant identity, the juvenile justice system had taught them only to act strategically in relation to the power structures that surrounded them.

Much like the teenagers in Chicago, Javon in Boston described his incarceration as a transformative moment. He believed that he had matured during his time at the Eliot Detention Center. "I am a lot calmer now than before." He thought that his life was going to be different after his release. "When I get out, I am just gonna lay low. Stay in the house more." He described disengaging from his friends as a major precondition for staying out of trouble. "I think I have to make myself stay away [from them]; otherwise bad things will happen." His plan was to finish his GED and get a job, but he was not sure what kind of job he would like to get. "Something outside; I could do an outside job."

Javon believed that the most important thing he had learned at the Eliot Detention Center was discipline. "They give you discipline in here," he said, adding, "When you do something, you get to feel the consequences right away, and then you think, 'I should have never done that.' Maybe on the outside I'll think about that more. I'll think about that I'll never wanna get back here." While he was at the Eliot Detention Center, Javon learned how to play by the rules. Most of the time he was classified as a level 4, the highest level that the teenagers could reach for good behavior. He was proud of himself for not getting into fights and remaining at level 4 for almost his whole time there. "I like being on level 4. It feels good; you get to do more stuff," he explained.

Javon pointed to a crucial aspect of being at a juvenile justice facility. A juvenile detention or treatment center is a completely artificial environment. Deviant acts are immediately followed by consequences. The knowledge that the punishment was certain made it easy for most teenagers to follow the rules. Needless to say, on the outside, actions and consequences were usually more disconnected. As the teenagers well knew, it was possible, if not likely, to get away with committing crimes. Disobedience on the outside was a gamble, a risk that may be worth taking. Unsurprisingly, while many of the teenagers did well when they were under constant supervision, once released, they were unable to stay away from the streets in the long term.

Javon's case also demonstrated how fast boredom set in once a teenager was sent back home. In total Javon had spent over a year and a half in DYS custody when he was finally released in January 2013. In the meantime his mother had moved out of Dorchester to a quieter suburb. When I interviewed him two weeks later, he seemed bored but relaxed. I thought he had grown in height, but I quickly realized that it was his demeanor that had changed. He was walking upright rather than with his shoulders hunched over. "I am just chillin', in there," he told me. "I was just stuck and all I thought about was negative stuff. Right now I am just trying to find something positive to get into." During our last meeting, at the end of March 2013, he had not found anything that could have set him on a positive path of desistance. In the meantime he had also been sent back to a DYS facility because he was caught hanging out in Boston with his old friends. "I am just bored," he explained. "I need friends. I don't know anyone out here. I am just sitting in the house all day, watching TV. I have no friends, no job, nothing."

His inability to find something worthwhile to do signified the limits of agency the teenagers experienced after their release. While the young men were incarcerated, every aspect of their lives was focused on getting out. They were bored, but their imagined desistance also made their time meaningful. Once the teenagers were back in their old environment, it became obvious that incarceration had not prepared them to take their life in their own hands.

Demarco was held in the same institutions as Javon. He had been arrested for armed robbery in November 2011. Sixteen at the time, he lived with his mother, father, and three-year-old sister in Dorchester. His parents had emigrated from the Caribbean and owned the home they lived in. Demarco was, according to his own assessment, constantly on the move. "I am just not a house person. I don't like being inside." He loved his neighborhood and enjoyed being part of street life even more. When I asked him why he liked Dorchester, he replied, "I like everything about it, the environment, the people, the drama. It's amazing stuff that's happening. It's like a movie in Dorchester."

Demarco had been on probation for several months already when he committed the robbery. He admitted that getting money was the most important motivation behind his actions. Demarco did not feel guilty for what he had done. "I don't regret it, nah. I regret it because I ended up back in here. But it happens every day that someone takes something from someone." While he was held in the pretrial detention center, he was hoping that his judge would give him another chance. He believed that this time he would be able to stay out of trouble. "I don't want to come back, because I am tired of my mom coming in here and visiting me. Also, I would have been off probation in December. I am just going to be in school and in the house. It is getting cold anyway." He knew, though, that he would most likely have to spend a long time in DYS custody. Demarco's charges were serious. He had not only violated his probation but also committed a second armed robbery.

In December 2012 he was indeed sentenced to spend a year at the John J. Connelly Youth Center. Like the other teenagers in the study, Demarco was certain that the risk of having to go back there would be sufficient to make him change his life. "I am done," he said; "I wanna be free." Demarco was finally released in January 2013. When I met up with him at the beginning of February, he told me that he had been doing well. He admitted that he smoked marijuana, but since he did not have to submit to urine testing, he did not think it was going to be a problem. When I asked him what had helped him to stay out of trouble in the past few weeks, he replied, "Remembering where I just came from. Just thinking about my freedom."

For all the youths enrolled in this study, being incarcerated fostered a desire to desist from crime. Unfortunately, relying on the negative experience of incarceration as a motivation for staying away from crime was insufficient to put the young men on a viable pathway of desistance. Lamar, for example, was placed at a camplike facility after his stay at the Eliot Detention Center. He indicated that he did not take the treatment program seriously. From his perspective, he gained nothing from being sent away from home: "I am just doing my time and then get out of here." Again, staying out of trouble was something he thought could be achieved easily. "It [doing the right thing] is not going to be hard. If I set my mind to it that I am gonna do something, then I am gonna do it." He believed that he was the only one to blame for his incarceration. He had committed crimes "because I didn't care; I wasn't thinking; I wasn't using my head." Despite his initial conviction to stay out of trouble, Lamar returned to a DYS treatment facility a few months after his release. He had been arrested again for carrying a gun.

Of all the Boston teenagers, Tyrell framed incarceration as a positive life event most explicitly. "When you are locked up, your mind is changing. Say, if I had the money to pay for the drugs I was supposed to sell, I would have not been caught and I would have got another package. I would have kept going. It is a chance for me. I am not trying to go back to DYS after I am out." Like Lamar, however, Tyrell also had to return to a DYS treatment facility. He violated his parole requirements, missed curfews, and failed to attend school. After being on the run for over five months to evade a warrant for his arrest, he was sentenced to spend another four months in DYS custody.

NARRATIVES OF INCARCERATION IN BOSTON AND CHICAGO

The narratives the teenagers developed while they were held in juvenile justice facilities were remarkably consistent across both field sites. Kendrick's case most clearly demonstrated the discrepancy between the teenagers' actual life on the outside and their imagined future. The only concrete strategy he had developed was staying away from his gang-member friends. He expected himself to recommit to schooling, even though he had never attended school regularly. Joining Job Corps was only a vague plan. He was unlikely to get into the program anytime soon. Kendrick's idea of leaving Illinois and moving to Texas was even more arbitrary. It was not Texas that attracted him, but the prospect of leaving his past behind.

Darrius's response, on the other hand, showed that the turning-point narrative would lose its plausibility if incarceration was experienced repeatedly. Since Darrius had witnessed his failure to follow through with his resolutions several times, being locked up became meaningless. Juvenile prison was not deterring him from committing new crimes or from disregarding his probation requirements. Instead, he seemed to have accepted incarceration as an inevitable part of his life course.

All the teenagers believed—at least initially—that the incarceration experience was going to be powerful enough to force them to do all the things they had never done successfully before. Incarceration set in motion the desire to reinvent themselves. The young men believed that their transformation could be achieved only through their own agency. Just as they had committed crimes because they had been "stupid," they would simply be smarter and "do the right thing" in the future.

This narrative allowed the teenagers to imagine their marginalized position as only temporary, an insignificant obstacle to their becoming successful adults. None of the teenagers used poverty or discrimination as an excuse for their criminal past. They explicitly blamed themselves, not their social circumstances. This strategy was not empowering, but rather exacerbated the misconceptions teenagers had about desistance and their future in American society. Most teenagers left juvenile justice facilities to return to the exact same environment they had come from. Fundamentally, nothing in this environment had changed, and, as they soon realized, neither had they.

INCARCERATION AS A DEFECTIVE TURNING POINT

Turning points that facilitate desistance usually allow for a "knifing off" of the past from the present. They are also supposed to be an opportunity for the development of new personal relationships that offer "support, growth, and new social networks" while changing the structure of routine activities. These contingent structural conditions are meant to open up space for transformative action and identity redefinition (Sampson and Laub 2005, 33–34). Finally, a turning point can fulfill its transformative potential only if the actor takes advantage of opportunities offered and actively participates in the creation of his or her new identity (Giordano, Cernkovich, and Rudolph 2002; Vaughan 2007; Gadd and Farrall 2004).

Incarceration in the juvenile justice system formally fulfills the structural conditions of turning points. The rehabilitative structures of juvenile justice facilities, such as the presence of social workers and therapists and of educational opportunities, encouraged the young men to reflect on their lives and to develop new, positive habits such as regular school attendance. The teenagers were also embedded in different networks and forced to alter their daily routine. From the teenagers' point of view, being incarcerated felt like a turning point because that assumption was structurally plausible. On the other hand, incarceration was an artificial experience, disconnected from the social processes surrounding the teenagers in their home environment (Carlsson 2012).

Exercising self-control in the face of restrictions may be a necessary but is not a sufficient condition for creating a viable nondeviant self. Making choices and building one's future creatively are essential parts of transforming the initial cognitive readiness for change into a successful turning point that can lead to long-term desistance from crime.

CONCLUSION: BELIEVING IN A BETTER FUTURE

Incarceration generated the impression of individual change without offering concrete opportunities to enact a life without crime. Juvenile justice facilities fostered an imagined desistance firmly connected to the narrative of the "American Dream." The young men almost intuitively adopted a language of agency and individual responsibility. Believing that they were the masters of their future resonated with the assumption that American society offers the same chances to everyone regardless of their socioeconomic background or skin color. While the teenagers were incarcerated, they did not take into account their structural constraints. They emphasized that it was completely in their hands to make a better life for themselves. Focusing on their agency allowed them to give meaning to their incarceration (Leverentz 2014; Maruna 2001). Thinking about their stay in a juvenile justice facility as a turning point not only eased the emotional pain of being away from friends and family but also gave them hope that they could be upwardly mobile despite their criminal past.

The teenagers' imagined desistance not only contradicted empirical evidence in this and previous studies (Gatti, Tremblay, and Vitaro 2009; Laub and Sampson 2003). Incarceration also generated the impression of a turning point without offering real alternatives for action after the teenagers were released. As the young men conceptualized their lives without crime, they were not driven by the hope of a positive reengagement with life on the outside. Rather, the trauma of incarceration was supposed to serve as a motivation for exercising self-control and forming habits that they had never successfully formed before.

From a life-course perspective, incarceration formally fulfilled the structural condition of a turning point. At the same time, it was a temporary, superimposed experience with almost no connection to the young men's social reality. Without being anchored in positive social experiences of nondeviance, imprisonment could not provide opportunities for creative self-transformation. The teenagers developed unrealistic expectations about their future and blamed themselves when they suffered rather predictable setbacks.

5 Weak Ties—Strong Emotions

CARING FOR JUVENILE OFFENDERS IN BOSTON AND CHICAGO

Darell had been angry a lot over the past few weeks. He felt misunderstood by his DCF caseworker and his probation officer. More than that, he didn't care for the group home he currently lived in. "It's not my home," he said, "and these people are not my family members." Whether they were family members or not, Darell was surrounded by people who were supposed to care for him. He had a probation officer, a DCF caseworker, and a social worker. Darell and his mother also saw a family therapist.

When I visited him at his Dorchester group home in early September 2012, Darell was about forty-five minutes late for our interview. I passed the time sitting in the dining area and talking to several staff members. They complained to me that Darell had not been following the house rules. One social worker suspected that he had stolen the iPhone he had been carrying around. She told me Darell had been late coming back from school almost daily, and she believed he had lied about where he had been. Darell knew how the staff saw him: "They think I am sneaky." The feeling of mistrust was mutual. "If you are told that they don't trust you in [to] your face, then you don't trust them either," he said. Darell drew a clear distinction between people who were assigned to care for him and his family members, who, he believed, knew him, understood him, and were truly interested in his well-being: "They [staff] don't put me on this earth. . . . I imagine by the time I am old, . . . I won't even remember half the people I know [now], but I guess while they are in my life I just have to deal with them."

Whether or not Darell was trustworthy may have been up for debate. More important analytically, however, is his distinction between people whom the state of Massachusetts had assigned to care for him and his family. Family connections represented open-ended, noninstrumental relationships and durable ties. Adults who worked for the juvenile justice system, on the other hand, were in his opinion unable to grasp the complexity of his life. "They think they know because they have done the work for so long, but I am different," he said, adding, "My situation is different than the other kids. They don't know me."

The relationships between professionals working for the juvenile justice system and teenage offenders were difficult to manage for both sides. Social workers and probation officers tended to be overworked and underpaid. Teenagers were aware that their social ties to juvenile justice professionals were not only fleeting but also framed by a fundamental power imbalance. The inability to establish mutuality during interactions is ingrained in the institutional framework of any bureaucracy (Weber 1979). This lack of mutuality is exacerbated in the US welfare system. In a system designed to ensure compliance rather than provide subsidiary help for moving out of poverty, providers and clients hardly meet as equals (Soss, Fording, and Schram 2011; Piven and Cloward 1993).

In Chicago and Boston the inequality between teenagers and juvenile justice professionals went further than institutionally entrenched power dynamics; it also manifested in racial and socioeconomic differences between the two parties (Platt 1977). In the end, the young men I interviewed shared the distinct impression that they couldn't rely on anyone but themselves to create a new life. Believing in their own agency despite confinement, poverty, and lack of education was the only way the young men could imagine ever overcoming their marginalized position.

INSTITUTIONALLY EMBEDDED INEQUALITY

Miguel in Chicago was frustrated with his probation officer and the programs he was supposed to participate in. In the first few weeks after his release from the Saura Center, Miguel lived with his grandfather in a small working-class town close to the Indiana border. Miguel was Latino but also had American Indian ancestry. His grandfather was part Navajo and the small, dark house was decorated with American Indian art that I assumed to be symbols of his Navajo heritage. Miguel was a gang member. During our first interview in April 2011 he admitted that he felt empowered by his connection to the Spanish Gangster Disciples (SGDs). He struggled to find words for the fleeting charisma he thought was associated with being an SGD: "Just to be known as somebody besides my name. Just to be known [as somebody] from this crew." He paused and added: "Skip your crew. F' your crew. This my crew. We [are] the best crew out here. We [are] the best people out here."

Miguel had never been arrested for a gang-related crime. He was sent to the juvenile detention center and later to the Saura Center because he physically attacked his mother during a fight. Despite his vocal commitment to his old gang life, Miguel established a new identity quickly after his release. He enrolled in an alternative high school without his probation officer's (PO's) knowledge. With his mother's help Miguel also found work in a downtown fast-food restaurant. In the meantime, his PO barely kept track of him and at times relied on me to run interference when he wanted Miguel to show up in court. Domestic violence was the only charge on Miguel's record, and his PO didn't know anything about his past gang involvement. Unsurprisingly, Miguel was convinced that his probation officer didn't understand which program would be most helpful for him. As he put it, "He doesn't really know me like that. He just knows me from my paperwork."

Miguel was aware that he was only one of many cases his PO had to deal with. He initially tried to get in touch with him to work out different living arrangements. Miguel didn't want to stay at his grandfather's house, which had little room for him and his belongings. When he was unable to reach his PO for several days, Miguel concluded that his probation officer was not interested in any deeper engagement. Indeed, Miguel's probation officer was eager to get him off his balance sheet. Before we were called in to see the judge at what turned out to be Miguel's final court date, his probation officer sternly expressed his dissatisfaction with Miguel. Miguel had not been attending school regularly and had refused to hand over his cell phone in school. He had also missed several appointments at his mandatory Evening Reporting Center. Nevertheless, once we were in the courtroom, the probation officer recommended the termination of Miguel's probation. He mentioned none of the infringements and instead praised Miguel's achievements, such as his job at the fast-food restaurant. When the judge decided to take Miguel off probation, Miguel seemed as surprised as I was by this outcome. Miguel had been irritated that his PO showed little interested in him, but in the end he also profited from the PO's carelessness. After all, he had been able to follow his own agenda, and he got off probation quickly.

Miguel's case was an exception, though. He was close to his family and had a social network that he could lean on outside the juvenile justice system. Other teenagers were less fortunate. In five Chicago cases, relatives transferred custody rights to the state while the teenagers were detained in the JTDC or the Saura center. The specific reasons varied across the cases, but mostly the families were sick of their sons, grandsons, nephews, or brothers bringing the police to their door. Those teenagers in particular who had no home to go back to after their release demanded a degree of attention and understanding that few POs or caseworkers were able to provide.

Ben, for example, felt judged and misunderstood by his DCFS caseworker. Ben had been a ward of the state for several years, but his relationship with his caseworker became strained after he entered adolescence. The previous five years Ben had been living on and off with his great-aunt Jane in Chicago's South Shore neighborhood. Jane was fairly well-off. She owned a three-story building containing two apartments that she shared with Ben and his little sister. The siblings had their own apartment on the first floor, while Jane lived on the second floor. Ben acknowledged that he had lacked for nothing materially or even emotionally since he moved in with Jane. Yet his great-aunt explained that Ben had always longed for his mother's love and approval. She felt for him because his mother, as she put it, "abandoned him and he never got the love a child deserves." Jane recalled that Ben's mother had no interest in engaging with him. On the few visits she paid her children, she was eager to play with Ben's little sister but usually ignored her son. She would send money to her daughter but put nothing in the envelope for Ben. Ben also adored his father. He had lived with him before he moved in with his great-aunt. As Jane told me, the two were very close, but his father, who reputedly had thirteen children with different women and was in and out of prison, hardly counted as a reliable role model.

When Ben started getting into trouble as a teenager, Jane, who was in her mid-sixties and struggled with a heart condition, couldn't handle the stress anymore. She asked DCFS to place Ben in another foster home. In reality Ben continued to spend most of his time at his great-aunt's house. Although he worked with his caseworker for years, he never felt close to her. Their relationship worsened when he was arrested for possession of a gun in the spring of 2010. Ben couldn't shake the impression that she had completely given up on him. "My caseworker said I was doing all this bad stuff, when I really wasn't doing it, so I actually started doing it. . . . I can't talk to her about that. I can't. She won't let me tell her. Every time I try to explain that to her, she says, she ain't listening. And then she compares me to her other clients. Just because I did some of the stuff they did, I am not like them."

The relationship teenagers have with juvenile justice personnel is comparable to that between a client and his or her therapist, or between a nanny and the family she or he works for. In both situations, a service is rendered that is not easily quantifiable in monetary terms (Simmel 2011; Zelizer 1997). In a therapeutic relationship, for example, the service offered and paid for often extends beyond the boundaries of an individual therapy session. Calling a therapist during off-hours, or assuming that a nanny not only feeds and clothes one's children but is also affectionate with them, is a reasonable expectation for middle-class clients to have. For the teenagers, however, the support they can expect is limited to their enrollment in specific juvenile justice programs. Once the often short-term intervention ends, they may never see that particular social worker, therapist, or probation officer again.

The teenagers were aware that, rather than being treated and assessed as individuals, they were one of many cases on a probation officer's or caseworker's balance sheet. Even an extraordinary engaged probation officer cannot provide the type of open-ended support a struggling teenager may need. Jamal's PO, for example, visited his family regularly and enrolled Jamal in a mentoring program. When Jamal's family refused to let him move back home, the PO visited him at his group home and took him out for lunch. Yet, when the PO went on vacation, Jamal, who in the meantime had recidivated and was held at the JTDC, felt abandoned. When I met Jamal at the detention center, he was visibly upset because his probation officer had not been in touch with him during the previous few weeks. "Larry does not care about me," he said. Since his PO usually went out of his way to attend to Jamal, he had developed expectations that exceeded the usual connection between probation officer and client. Jamal's demands of constant attention were similar to what a child might expect from his parent, and they contravened the professional relationship the probation officer aspired to maintain despite his commitment to helping Jamal.

The gray zone of purchasing the nonquantifiable good of emotional support is made more frustrating by the fact that the teenagers have no leverage over the service provider (Weber 1979; Blau 1986). Whereas juvenile justice personnel approach the young men from a professional distance, the teenagers depend on them not only to secure their freedom but also for access to other desirable social services, such as clothing vouchers and employment opportunities. Unlike a therapist who is paid by his or her client, the youths do not directly partake in a monetary exchange relationship. The probation officer may theoretically depend on the occurrence of juvenile delinquency to remain employed, but his salary does not decrease or increase in relation to any individual teenager. The teenagers had neither economic nor social capital with which to influence the outcome of a particular interaction (Bourdieu 1984).

The biggest challenge for the young men in Boston was to openly engage in therapeutic interventions. Tyrell, for example, struggled to build a trusting relationship with his DYS caseworker. He was overwhelmed with his DYS requirements and in the end was on the run for almost four months before he was recommitted to a DYS treatment center. Reflecting on why he recidivated, Tyrell said he had not communicated well with his caseworker about what was on his mind. "I did not realize how helpful they were. I thought they were just about, you violated, you'll get locked up. . . . I just did not get the part, where if I needed help I could go to them. . . . I felt like, 'Damn, if I go to them, what if they pull me in for that?'" Even teenagers who attributed goodwill to their caseworkers took an instrumental approach to their interactions. The caseworker was perceived as a "manager," rather than an individual who could be trusted and would provide emotional support. Asked what his caseworker did for him, Lamar replied, "Getting me a job, finding me community service, keeping me busy." Demarco emphasized that he talked to his caseworker only when he "needs to get things done." Moreover, he commented, "I am trying not to get too comfortable with him. I am just trying to do what I have to until I age out [of the DYS]."

Even if a teenager successfully established mutuality and trust with a social worker, staff member, or clinician, this relationship was not likely to last beyond his stay in a particular facility. Teenagers who were committed to the DYS in Boston usually encountered three different clinicians during their time in detention and treatment facilities. Every time they relocated to a different institution, they also confronted a new set of therapeutic personnel. Having to leave individuals behind with whom they had connected often led to an initial rejection of the new clinician.

Javon's case illustrates the tendency for youths to assume they had to be on guard when they interacted with juvenile justice personnel. Tall and heavyset, Javon had a friendly demeanor and was pleasant to talk to. Before his arrest, he lived with his mother in Roxbury close to the Franklin Park Zoo. Javon had one half-brother on his mother's side and several siblings on his father's side with whom he was in touch. He described his half-brother as the exact opposite of him. His brother always liked school and was very athletic. While Javon awaited the outcome of his trial at Eliot Detention Center, his brother attended Brandeis University on an athletic scholarship.

On the outside Javon spent a lot of time at his grandmother's place while his mother was working. Mostly he was hanging out with two other boys who lived close to his grandmother's house. He did not go into detail about his past, but just said that he was out on the street "doing stuff." Javon explained that he never saw himself as being in a gang. The people he hung with on the outside were friends to whom he felt very close, as if they were family. In late spring 2011 he was arrested for carrying a gun. Javon told me that he was carrying the weapon "for protection." Over the two years I met with him, I never felt threatened or even uncomfortable. He was always one of the teenagers I looked forward to speaking with.

The juvenile justice system had a very different perception of him. When Javon's judge eventually established that the police officers had probable cause to search him, Javon was committed for nine months to the John J. Connelly Youth Center, the most secure facility for juveniles in the Boston area. After one of my visits, a staff member told me that he considered Javon the most dangerous youth they were currently housing. He believed that all the other inmates were afraid of him because they knew what he was capable off. When I asked Javon about his street life and his reputation during one of our next meetings, he just shrugged his shoulders and replied, "It's irrelevant if they can't prove anything, isn't it?"

After a few months in the John J. Connelly Center, Javon's street life began to catch up with him. His best friend died in a gang-related shooting. A few weeks later he talked about it for the first time. "He didn't deserve it. He was only twenty. I used to be with him every day." Javon also admitted that he was angry, and he told me that he struggled with thoughts of taking revenge after his release. When I asked him whether he had talked to his clinician about this, he vehemently replied, "No! I can't talk to them about that. If I tell them, they think I am gonna do it [take revenge], even though I am not. I am just thinking about it." He missed the clinician he had talked to at the detention center: "I like her better than all of the other clinicians. We were just building a relationship when I was locked up in there [Eliot Detention Center]." Given the rehabilitative mission of the juvenile justice system in Boston, staff should have provided support precisely in situations that put teenagers' fragile nondeviant identities in jeopardy. Nevertheless, Javon had the impression that his true feelings would be held against him later on if he expressed them now. Without anyone he considered trustworthy, he decided that it was best to keep his thoughts to himself and to work through his emotions alone.

Like Javon, Jason, in Boston, also had to leave a clinician behind whom he felt close to when he was released from his treatment center. As he was reintegrating into the community, he was forced to see a therapist that he didn't care for very much. According to Jason, he opened up to his clinician at the treatment center because they shared a same sense of humor. "I can actually laugh at her jokes. I could relate to her, 'cause she is sort of goofy. She is easy to talk to. She is like, 'What's the matter?' We would joke around. She is more like a best friend or something. The other one [the therapist on the outside] is just weird. The conversations we have are just weird." Jason also felt that, unlike his therapist on the outside, the clinician he had at his treatment center cared about him. "She said something like, 'If you need me, you can just talk to me.' That was kind of helpful." Jason's clinician broke through the bureaucratic barrier that tended to separate the teenagers from juvenile justice professionals. Using humor and emphasizing that her interest in Jason was genuine and more than just a job she had to do, she opened a space for mutuality and trust.

Establishing a close relationship also takes time. Demarco trusted his clinician because he had been working with her for years. She did not work for the DYS, but his petition to see her instead of a DYS clinician was granted, and he enjoyed working with her after he was released at the end of more than twelve months at John J. Connelly Youth Center. "She sees what's going on," Demarco said. "She is cool. I know her for like three years. When I get mad, she talks it out with me."

In Chicago, clinicians and therapists were not a regular feature of the teenagers' postincarceration life. Nor did they play a prominent role while the teenagers were held in detention facilities, group homes, or prisons. Trevor, in fact, was the only teenager who mentioned his art therapist, whom he had met while at the Saura Center. He asked to continue his therapy after his release. None of the other teenagers reported a sustained therapeutic engagement with a mental health care professional.

Probation officers and clinicians are institutionally restricted in their ability to establish a truly mutual relationship with their clients. One might even argue that mutuality, particularly between a PO and a client, is undesirable, the rationale being that the young men should learn to respect authority rather than becoming friendly with their PO. A professional distance is also necessary to achieve therapeutic success. Studies of the administration of cognitive behavioral therapy in a juvenile justice setting show that a collaborative understanding between clients and therapist is most likely reached when the staff take an objective stance and avoid favoritism, unreasonable punishment, or extreme lenience (Quinn and Shera 2009). From the perspective of a teenager, however, it was difficult to distinguish professional distance from a lack of care. For young men who were attuned to the punitive aspects of juvenile justice, it was therefore easier to maintain a façade of self-reliance.

RACIAL AND SOCIAL INEQUALITY

Waiting for a teenager attending a hearing at the Chicago juvenile court took a lot of patience. Relatives and friends often had to sit on uncomfortable wooden benches for hours until they were called into the courtroom. The crowd populating the hallways was easy to differentiate. Family and friends who were there to support a teenager tended to be African American or Latino. Those who worked for the juvenile justice department were usually white. In the months I spent waiting outside courtrooms, I saw few white families. During the recruitment process for this project I encountered only two white teenagers involved with the Chicago juvenile justice system. I met no white families in Boston. When I introduced myself to friends or relatives at the courthouse in Chicago, they assumed I was a probation officer or social worker.[1]

To my surprise, though, the teenagers in both cities did not focus on racial inequality when they described their relationships to juvenile justice personnel. They framed the social distance between themselves and the representatives of the juvenile justice system in socioeconomic terms. From the teenagers' perspective racial and socioeconomic inequality overlapped and were almost indistinguishable. They presupposed that being white was equivalent to being privileged. Racial inequality was such an omnipresent fact of life that it didn't even seem part of their conscious perception. Understanding their marginal position in terms of economic disadvantage, furthermore, allowed teenagers to hold on to the illusion of being able to leave their marginalized social position behind. Economic disadvantage can, theoretically at least, be overcome through hard work and self-discipline. Racial inequality, on the other hand, has more complex implications for upward mobility. Acknowledging a systematic disadvantage based on race ran counter to the teenagers' narrative of agency, responsibility, and self-reliance. The topic of racial inequality came up only when a crisis forced the teenagers to reevaluate their own limitations.[2]

In the weeks before our last interview in June 2013, Jason experienced several tragic events that wreaked havoc in his family. A cousin of was killed in a gang-related shooting. Jason had been about to leave the house to meet up with him when his cousin canceled abruptly. Later that day, Jason received a phone call telling him that his cousin had died. A few weeks afterward, his aunt, the cousin's mother, was found stabbed to death in her closet. Her husband was charged with the crime. In a moment when Jason had to deal with extreme tragedy, he expressed for the first time that his struggles were not just a function of his own mistakes but also a result of being African American. He told me: "I would honestly say that being out here, black people, it's like still being in Africa. 'Cause we're still in the struggle. We don't get it as worse as Africa, but there's a lot of blacks struggling right now." I had seen Jason handle challenging situations with ease, but losing three family members within a short time was too much for him. He started crying during our interview. The meaningless deaths of his cousin and aunt forced him to consider external forces that limited his ability to shape his own future.

Javon was the only youth who—at least implicitly—talked about how racial inequality affected his relationships with juvenile justice workers. Like Jason, he acknowledged racial inequality in a moment of extreme frustration. A white staff member at the John J. Connelly Youth Center had accused him of being disrespectful and had framed his actions as a refusal to rehabilitate himself. His assessment had consequences for the length of Javon's incarceration and the type of supervision he would have to deal with after his release. Javon claimed: "I didn't say anything. I [knew] I would have gotten into trouble [if I had]. Why would I do that? You are a white man, and you run the building. There is nothing I can do. There is nothing I am doing. They just want to find something!"

Javon implied that it would be utterly absurd to be disrespectful to a white man in such a powerful position. The power dynamic was so obvious to Javon that even the idea of getting into a verbal altercation with this person was inconceivable to him. Javon's acknowledgment of the racial inequality between staff and inmates remained the exception among the teenagers. More often they focused on the socioeconomic boundaries that separated them particularly from the therapeutic staff. The young men argued that clinicians and the programs they administered simply did not capture the reality of growing up in a crime-ridden, poverty-stricken urban neighborhood. Jason, for instance, felt that the advice he received during group therapy meetings at his treatment center was unhelpful. "Everything they are telling us in here has nothing to do with us getting out," he said. He explained how therapists walked them through scenarios designed to help them face challenging situations. He ultimately found those hypothetical scenarios unrealistic: "'Cause every moment we could walk down the street and we be like blah blah blah, I am not from this place no more, and a person would still shoot you."

Teenagers frequently perceived group therapy sessions as unhelpful. One-on-one interactions with staff who supervised them on the unit had a bigger impact on them. These men and women were present during all hours of the day and constantly remained in close proximity to the teenagers. A "youth service group worker" is an entry-level position at the DYS in Boston. Job advertisements list no general requirements except having a valid Massachusetts driver's license.[3] Staff who held these entry-level positions therefore often came from the same socioeconomic and racial background as the teenagers. Many had grown up in similar neighborhoods and had also been involved in street life when they were younger. Because of this shared history, the teenagers felt the line staff understood them. They took their advice seriously, even though staff working on the units exercised the most direct punitive control over them.

Despite his struggles with some of the staff members at his group home, Darell still perceived them as much more helpful than his clinician. "They cool. They can relate. They grew up in my environment. They understand. They can talk to me when I am making the wrong decisions." Demarco echoed this sentiment. Asked whether he talked to staff members at his treatment facility, he replied, "I talk to a couple of them. I mean, they know. They grew up the way we grew up." Tyrell even praised the staff at his treatment facility: "It's the coolest staff here. They'll help you out. They really care for you."

The Chicago teenagers shared similar sentiments. While he was held at the Saura Center, Trevor established a close relationship with one of the men who worked there. He reported that he even stayed in touch after his release. "I trust him. I talked to him a lot. I'd be calling him at the Saura Center to thank him for helping me to change and everything." James reported that staff members also cut teenagers some slack and would not immediately write up infringements. He recalled a violent encounter with one of his fellow inmates that several staff members witnessed:

> It was at the Saura Center; I was just about to leave to go to court, and we were in the little waiting room after we eat lunch. He [the fellow inmate] just kept calling me a bitch, and I told him, "I don't like that. Don't call me bitch." He got all into my face, so I pushed him off of me. He punched me in the jaw, so I picked him up. He is a skinny guy, so I just picked him up and I slammed him on his head. Nobody tried to stop it. They just kept going [about their business]. They said, "Oh, well, you might as well finish fighting 'cause you gonna get locked up now."

Yet the staff members who were present did not report the incident. As James recalled, "They told us, 'If Mike [director of the Saura Center] or anybody asks you, just say no fists were thrown; you guys were just wrestling.' We said all right and that was that."

While such acts of lenience may encourage youths to trust staff members, it also opens the door to inconsistent decision making and favoritism. Indeed teenagers in Chicago perceived their negative interactions with staff members mostly in terms of unreliability, favoritism, and rule-related inconsistencies. Jamal, for example, believed that the staff members at his temporary group home were misleading him and not rewarding him adequately for helping them clean up the house. James admitted that the staff at his group home made him angry because they changed the rules of the house arbitrarily. "They are making up new rules like every week. I just don't say anything. Just walk away and go outside or something." He also had the impression that some staff members did not pay attention. One staff member in particular, James felt, "talked too much." He elaborated: "If you try to talk to him, he don't listen. He don't listen and he don't let you talk. He is always sarcastic."[4]

Nevertheless, some teenagers identified with staff to such an extent that they viewed working with juvenile offenders as a viable career option. When asked about his future plans, Tyrell explained that he wanted to work as a counselor to teenagers. "I wanna help kids in the future." He went on: "I want them to know what I have been through so that they don't go through that path, you know. That's what I wanna do." Staff members who occupied entry-level positions gave the teenagers an idea of what having a stable income and benefits could look like. Especially African American teenagers hardly knew any other men who were able to make a living wage in the official labor market (A. Goffman 2014; Wilson 2009; Western 2006). The teenagers also felt qualified to do the work. After all, they had spent years navigating the system. Imagining themselves as helping other youth likely also allowed them to give meaning to their time otherwise lost in juvenile facilities (Maruna, Wilson, and Curran 2006).

When the institutionally enforced power imbalance was exacerbated by social and racial inequality, interactions between juvenile offenders and juvenile justice professionals became increasingly difficult to manage. The social distance between the juvenile offenders on one hand and caseworkers, clinicians, and probation officers on the other was large and their lives intersected only within the institutional framework of juvenile justice. From the teenagers' perspective, the programs they had to participate in and the clinicians they had to talk to often symbolized upper-middle-class ignorance about their upbringing (Platt 1977). Teenagers could easily dismiss interventions as being unrelated to their lifeworld.

Entry-level juvenile justice workers were more likely than most clinicians, caseworkers, and POs to transcend the power imbalance inherent in the bureaucratic structure of the juvenile justice system. Their ability to refer to a shared past allowed them to reach beyond their institutionally prescribed role. The continuous contact staff members had with the teenagers also contributed to a breakdown in social barriers. With no offices they could retreat to, line staff were around the youths all day. At the same time, relationships built on a shared biography were not without drawbacks. Those connections could also become problematic when arbitrary decision making sneaked into the day-to-day processes of juvenile justice facilities. Entry-level staff members were socially closer to the teenagers than to the administrative leadership of the facilities. They were doing the hard work of handling the young men day in and day out. Guidelines and staff handbooks could not capture the messy reality of simultaneously managing rehabilitation and punishment. Entry-level staff members therefore had to improvise as they tried to fulfill the multiple and often contradictory missions of juvenile justice (Zimring 2005). Lenience and the more problematic favoritism at the bottom of the bureaucratic hierarchy thus seem almost unavoidable in the otherwise highly stratified organizational structure of juvenile justice.

CONCLUSION: POWER, INTERACTION, AND RECIDIVISM

The data reveal many similarities between Boston and Chicago. Yet there were significant differences between the two field sites as well. The teenagers in Chicago, for example, did not report consistent interactions with mental health professionals. Chicago teenagers also had the impression that they were dealing with a one-size-fits-all approach, because their probation officers or caseworkers did not have to get to know them better, or neglected to take the time.

Boston youths struggled to understand the position of their caseworker, who fulfilled a problematic dual role. Caseworkers were responsible for revoking parole when necessary, but they were also supposed to be supportive should teenagers struggle on the outside. In contrast to Chicago, in Boston, teenagers had to meet with multiple adults who sought their attention. Teenagers therefore exercised triage. They approached some relationships in purely instrumental ways and weighed the cost of opening up and "telling their story" in the limited time they spent with a particular individual. Thus, while teenagers in Chicago were often unable to establish trust because they lacked sustained attention from juvenile justice workers, the Boston youths tended to be overwhelmed by the multiplicity of interactions required of them.

In both cities the teenagers understood that people who were charged with supporting them could also restrict their freedom at any time. Max Weber defined power as the "chance of a man or a number of men to realize their own will in a communal action even against the resistance of others who are participating in the action" (Weber 1958, 180). The punitive bureaucracy that surrounded the relationships between teenagers and juvenile justice representatives generated an ideal situation for one group's unconditional ability to exercise power over another group (Weber 1949; Weber 1979). The young men's reintegration into the community depended on probation officers, caseworkers, and clinicians whose reports and assessments directly influenced when and how they were allowed to go home. The teenagers were therefore engaged in unilateral relationships that "are the penultimate source of power" (Blau 1986, 22).

Racial and socioeconomic differences further amplified the institutional inequality. Probation officers, caseworkers, and clinicians were middle-class professionals. Many of the teenagers came from extremely disadvantaged families. It was easier for them to build rapport with entry-level juvenile justice workers, many of whom knew the streets. The teenagers felt these workers understood them on a fundamental level. On the other hand, they also exercised direct punitive control over the young men. Every day, line staff had to face the complex reality of controlling and simultaneously rehabilitating youths (Haney 2010). Social proximity and being in close quarters with each other led to arbitrary rule enforcement and favoritism. In the end all relationships the teenagers built were temporary and ceased to exist once the young men left a specific program.

Despite the fraught nature of these connections, the young men wanted and also needed adults in their life who cared for them and helped them to build a nondeviant identity. From a life-course perspective, establishing new social connections that lead away from deviance is important for long-term desistance from crime (Sampson and Laub 2005; Laub and Sampson 2003). Creating conditions in which trusting relationships can be established would therefore likely improve juvenile justice outcomes. In reality, the teenagers mostly relied on themselves to rebuild a life without crime. Their families had either turned their backs on them or even presented obstacles to desistance. Believing in their own agency therefore allowed the teenagers to compensate for their inability to trust and build mutual relationships with the adults in their lives.

Knowing that they likely would not have a lasting impact on the teenagers' lives, many juvenile justice professionals reinforced this narrative of agency and self-reliance. "He needs to just stay away from the streets"; "He just has to focus on school"; and "He needs to work on his anger" were phrases that POs and social workers repeated like mantras. Focusing on agency fed into the teenagers' natural desire to believe in a better future. Yet it did little to prepare them for the failure, poverty, and discrimination they would likely experience after their release.

Juvenile justice professionals were aware that once the teenagers went back to the community, all bets were off. A clinician in Boston explained to me how months of therapy and rehabilitation could be quickly erased once teenagers returned to their old neighborhood: "We have some kids that are back here after three days and they don't even know how it happened. They just went out, had a wild night, and then end up back here." The teenagers' problems simply could not be solved by individual adults who intersected with their lives only briefly. The relationships between juvenile justice professionals and teenagers, rather, re-created the structural and racial inequalities in which the youths had been socialized from birth.

6 The Uncertainty of Freedom

TEENAGERS' DESIRE FOR CONFINEMENT
AND SUPERVISION

Lucas's situation was complicated. I met him at the Eliot Detention Center, where he was being held for armed robbery. He was released fairly quickly and spent most of the year and a half during which we met regularly on the outside. While he was on juvenile probation, one of his associates pressed charges against him. His former friend claimed that Lucas had threatened him and his pregnant girlfriend. New accusations followed, and the whole case became an increasingly confusing he said–she said scenario. Lucas insisted vehemently that the allegations were unfounded. The details were far too complex to be recounted here, but it seemed to boil down to a fistfight over ten dollars that Lucas had borrowed. Lucas was already seventeen when the charges were filed, so he went to trial in the adult criminal justice system.

At first, Lucas had to wear an ankle bracelet as a condition of his juvenile probation. After a brief intermission the bracelet was reinstated to monitor his movements during his adult trial. At the beginning of his juvenile probation he was also on home confinement. For several months he could leave the house only to go to school. Lucas lived a tenuous life. He knew that his release was only conditional, and the constant supervision wore him out emotionally and physically. Nevertheless, he insisted that probation was no more than a "slap on the wrist." He argued that being supervised helped him to stay out of trouble, because he was forced to remain in the house at night. Without probation and the ankle bracelet, he said, he would probably have been caught for something worse. Lucas believed that he was lucky: "I know people that learned lessons the hard way. They're either dead or they're doing life right now."

As his adult trial dragged on, it became more difficult for Lucas to keep up this positive perspective. Pondering the possibility of an adult conviction, he expressed frustration with the time and money he had lost: "I had five months of my life taken away to a freaking bracelet. One month taken away from my life doing time. It builds up . . . I don't ever get that piece back." Although he vented such frustrations more frequently, he kept reminding himself that it could be worse. The ankle bracelet, he believed, had given him the space to mature and protected him from getting involved even more deeply in the streets.

Lucas also used probation as an excuse to exit social situations that could lead to involvement in illegal behavior (Goffman 2014). During one of our later interviews, he described a situation at a friend's house that had the potential of boiling over. The other teenagers he hung out with were looking for trouble by teasing passersby. Lucas elaborated: "A car passed by. [The passengers were] like, what the fuck, you wanna fight? And stuff like that. Stuff I would do when I was younger . . . immature stuff. So I was like, I'm sorry bro, but I can't chill with y'all. Y'all are hot."

While Lucas worked hard to give his restrictions a positive spin, the pressures the ankle bracelet put on him continued to mount. He was supposed to stay away from the street his former associates lived on. Unfortunately, his long-term girlfriend and his accuser lived in the same apartment building. Even if he had no intention to see the latter, the area was off-limits. Once, his bracelet came off while he was taking a subway line that passed close by the plaintiff's building. He immediately received a phone call warning him that he was in violation of his probation.

The bracelet also bothered Lucas when he was sleeping. He told me that one night he was so agitated that he started hitting it against the wall. He had recurring dreams about getting arrested again because he had missed his curfew. In the dream, "I got home at 9:30. But I was supposed [to be home earlier]. My curfew was at 8:30. So I looked at my watch, and my watch was broken . . . and it said 7:30. So I got home and I was like, what the hell. And they called me, and they were like, we have a warrant for your arrest. And I'm like, what the hell . . . my watch says 7:30."

Simple tasks like going to the doctor became difficult to navigate as well. After some blood tests indicated he had low iron levels, Lucas was scheduled to return for further evaluation and received medication. He couldn't reach his juvenile probation officer to get permission to leave the house and had to miss his doctor's appointment. The ankle bracelet was a constant reminder that that he could be pulled back into the detention center anytime. It was heavy, and because it fit loosely, it constantly rubbed against his ankle. Over the course of a day he needed to keep track of the remote control and its charge, because the bracelet needed to be recharged for two hours every day. Lucas usually crouched down close to a power outlet while he was watching TV. The list of problems and uncomfortable situations the bracelet caused became longer as time went on. The bracelet went off for no reason while he was working his retail job—a position he had obtained after months of job searching. He had to wear the ankle bracelet during his high school graduation. When he lost the charger, he had to pay for a new one.

ANKLE BRACELETS AND DESISTANCE

Despite the long list of hassles it entailed, the bracelet also simplified Lucas's life by removing from his daily routine potential opportunities for crime (Felson and Cohen 1979). Just as detention centers became familiar and even comfortable spaces for some teenagers, Lucas framed probation as a necessary evil that was a net positive for him. In the spring of 2013, as our meetings came to an end, he convinced himself that without the GPS monitor, he would have had more difficulty leaving the streets behind.

Before his arrest for armed robbery Lucas and his friends were deeply involved in Dorchester's street life. Lucas admitted that he used to rob people regularly. He and his friends snatched iPhones right out of pedestrians' hands. They had just never been caught. "I used to sell an iPhone like every day," Lucas told me. "I used to get like $280 every day. Split profit with my boy. I'll get $180, and he'll get $100 or something like that. . . . 'Cause I'll be the one that put in the work. . . . But he'll be the one to show me the ways. . . . He'll be the brains. I'll be the one doing it."

Lucas also told me that he was used to violence. When he visited his cousins in Puerto Rico, he witnessed execution-style shootings in broad daylight. One man got shot right next to him. Even in Boston, a comparably peaceful city, he saw people gunned down. Lucas vividly remembered one scene: "I was in middle school and I looked out the window. Some guy just ran up to some other guy and boom, boom—and then he ran. A group of people just ran to him, and he was like laying down, but I was like, did I just see that?"

Lucas's parents grew up in Puerto Rico, and even though the island is American soil, Lucas perceived it as a foreign country. He believed that the mainland United States offered more opportunities for upward mobility than Puerto Rico. He also thought that he was fortunate in having spent most of his childhood in Dorchester. "Nothing is worse than the part of Puerto Rico I am from," he said. He conceded that the United States was not perfect. If it were up to him, the rich would pay more in taxes, but compared to his Puerto Rican cousins, he had a lot of options.

Lucas's family lived in an apartment in West Roxbury. His block was a pocket of smaller, mostly working-classes houses in an area otherwise affluent. Their home was just a few minutes' drive from large mansions, exclusive clothing stores, and expensive suburban restaurants. His parents had moved out of the city because they wanted Lucas and his brother to stay out of trouble. The apartment was small and dark but very orderly. Lucas's father was much older than his mother. Already retired, he suffered from diabetes. He did not speak any English. His mother's English was broken but she could understand the basics. The salary she earned taking care of elderly people was essential for the family, and its economic situation became precarious when she had to stop working. Lucas's mother was diagnosed with breast cancer that turned out to be incurable. She underwent radiation therapy and suffered the horrendous side-effects. Lucas now needed to find a job, not only because he wanted to save up for his driver's license and a car, but also because he wanted to supplement the household income. The future of his immediate family was uncertain, and Lucas felt that he needed to step up.

Amidst this turmoil the ankle bracelet provided order and predictability. Lucas knew that he could not commit any crimes, because the probation department was able to determine his location at all times. The certainty of getting arrested if he made a misstep, he argued, made his desistance more manageable. During the time Lucas and I talked regularly, he did not recidivate. By the spring of 2013 he had been working for several months, obtained his driver's license, and saved up enough money to buy a used car. He was about to graduate from high school. The ankle bracelet had kept him off the streets until he seemed to have matured out of criminal behavior (Gottfredson and Hirschi 1990).

In terms of outcomes Lucas was indeed a success. The strong connection he had with his girlfriend helped him handle disappointments without losing track of his ultimate goals. He wanted to finish high school and become an auto mechanic. He persisted in his job search despite setbacks and hardly any support from his juvenile probation officer. In short, Lucas was an extremely self-sufficient teenager. Quite possibly, Lucas would have desisted from crime even without the ankle bracelet. His girlfriend wanted him to stay away from the streets, and his mother's deteriorating health forced him to reconsider his past actions, as well (Wakefield and Uggen 2010; Laub and Sampson 2003). While he considered being on probation helpful, he might have achieved even more if he had received nonpunitive support during his challenging transition to adulthood.

MISSED OPPORTUNITIES

From a public policy perspective, it does not matter whether Lucas reached his potential. Decisions about the future of specific juvenile justice interventions are based not on speculations about processes, but on outcomes. Recidivism rates in particular are the primary consideration determining the allocation of funds. The use of cognitive behavioral therapy (CBT) in the juvenile justice setting, for instance, has spread because this approach seems to drastically reduce recidivism rates (Landenberger and Lispey 2005). Unsurprisingly, DYS framed its own success or failure in terms of these numbers. DYS tracks youths' offending for twelve months after their release from a treatment facility. The earliest data available while I conducted my research were results from 2006. Of the male and female teenagers released in 2006, 34 percent were reconvicted within a year. This constituted a 5 percent increase from 2005. Despite its convenience and easy accessibility, this rudimentary statistic cannot effectively account for the contingent process of desistance or recidivism. The 66 percent of male teenagers who, according to the DYS, successfully desisted in 2006 may still have recidivated, but simply did not get caught. Focusing on outcomes also obscures social, economic, and emotional dimensions that can impact young men's future beyond the time period used as a cutoff for quantitative recidivism data.

My qualitative data cannot determine the causality of factors that contributed to Lucas's desistance, either. Yet I observed that Lucas, without any help from his probation officer, created positive experiences that helped him to construct a nondeviant self. Rather than monitoring him nonstop, juvenile justice and, later, the criminal justice system could have reinforced his ability to lead an autonomous life without crime. Instead, being on probation encouraged Lucas to think of himself as someone who lacks self-control. He embraced his confinement because he did not trust himself to stay away from the streets without a machine that tracked every movement he made. Ankle bracelets, in particular, mimicked the conditions of incarceration quite effectively. Teenagers whose movements were monitored round the clock also did not learn to make positive life choices without the certainty of punishment looming over them.

FICTITIOUS SUCCESS

During their probation or parole, the teenagers' understanding of success and failure continued to be determined within the parameters of the juvenile justice system. Many young men had never experienced positive reinforcement from any social institution other than the juvenile justice system. Treatment centers in Boston tried to give the teenagers the impression of success by holding art contests or awarding certificates for residents who followed the rules.

While Javon was held at the Eliot Detention Center, he received an award for remaining on the highest level for the longest time of any resident. "I like being on level 4," he said. "It feels good; you get to do more stuff." At the John J. Connelly Center he won an art contest and was proud of his achievement. "I drew a power-to-your-future picture. It was like a road and a candle, and on the side there was a band and it says: 'Empowerment. The time is now.' It basically means: 'You have a bright future.'" He had never won a contest before. While being incarcerated or being on probation may have been painful, some teenagers experienced success for the first time in their lives. These performances of accomplishment replaced actual credentials, however, and were meaningless outside the social boundaries of the juvenile justice setting the teenagers were embedded in (Fader 2013).

The regular performance of success is directly related to the widespread application of CBT in juvenile justice settings. The young men in Boston and Chicago constantly received rewards for good behavior. They were allowed to stay out of their rooms longer if they behaved well. Some Boston teenagers earned home passes. Many attended school regularly for the first time while they were detained, and their consistent attendance translated into good grades. Being on probation or parole, therefore, not only replicated the claustrophobic feeling of being incarcerated, but also re-created positive feelings of success that the teenagers enjoyed while they were held in juvenile justice institutions.

CBT is designed to change destructive thinking patterns and consequently to alter the actions an individual takes when a certain trigger appears. The teenagers in Boston and Chicago mostly recalled the "mindfulness" aspect of CBT, which is supposed to teach clients to respect themselves and others. In the teenagers' perception, "mindfulness" took on the meaning of self-control. Proponents of CBT maintain that, if CBT is applied correctly and in a sustained manner, behavior acquired in a therapeutic setting will transfer to the real world (Farmer and Chapman 2008). Much as Pavlov's dog salivated when the bell rang, the teenagers were supposed to activate the right thinking patterns when a trigger appeared, even without the presence of immediate rewards.

The social environment the young men returned to, indeed, did not offer many rewards for good behavior. Bad behavior was not immediately punished, either. Depending on a teenager's perceived likelihood of getting arrested, the reward structure could be reversed. As the teenagers confirmed, criminal behavior came with its own benefits: a rush of adrenalin, excitement, status, money (Katz 1988). The best-behaved resident at a detention center, on the other hand, was still not necessarily welcome at his neighborhood high school. In Boston and Chicago most teenagers continued to attend alternative schools, because they had exhausted their regular public school options. At home, familial problems, poverty, addiction, and illness awaited most of them. Probation, in contrast, replicated the artificial system of punishment and reward that was familiar to them. Complying with rules meant that curfews were extended or ankle bracelets removed.

Marvin did not think much beyond achieving these goals. He lived in one of the poorest areas on Chicago's West Side. His mother had so many children that Marvin couldn't keep track of how many siblings he had; a minimum of ten children lived in his home and the house was crawling with people. The family was poor in all the ways one might imagine. The house was falling apart. The older kids supervised the younger ones while their mother was working. Their front yard was filled with trash. The street they lived on was barely paved. With his limited vocabulary, Marvin mumbled and sometimes stopped speaking mid-sentence. He did not like to talk, but he also lacked the vocabulary to express himself. Marvin went to Healy North while he was on home confinement. He was one of the few students who did not live at the Saura Center while attending the alternative school. His main motivation to go to school regularly was "to make my papers look good, going to school and everything so that they let me off house arrest." Marvin was focused on getting off probation completely. He enjoyed staying out late, and it bothered him that he needed to be home by 10:00 on weekdays and 11:00 on weekends. If it had been up to him, Marvin would have spent all night outside, coming home around 2:00 or 3:00. He remained positive, though: "Once I get off probation," he said, "I can go back doing the same thing [staying out late with friends]."

During the summer of 2010 Marvin attended school regularly. He stayed in the house as he was supposed to, and his home confinement ended. Yet, once the incentive structure of the juvenile justice system was less tangible, Marvin was drawn again to the streets. Just a few weeks after his home confinement ended, I visited him in Cook County Jail, where he was held pretrial for armed robbery. As a seventeen-year-old he was now considered an adult.

Like Marvin, most teenagers were not well prepared for leading autonomous lives upon reaching certain milestones. Jason, for instance, admitted that he did well on the outside as long as he was on probation. Before his arrest for carrying a gun that led to his DYS commitment, being on probation stabilized his behavior: "I got on probation, then I was forced to go back to school. Probation kind of helped, then I got back on track in school," he explained. Yet, once he was off probation, he stopped attending school regularly.

Probation also helped James ignore the teasing from his Latino classmates. He was broad shouldered and, as a gang member, was used to responding with physical violence if he was disrespected. When he moved to a group home outside Chicago, he was one of the few Africa Americans at the school he attended. "Like, all the Mexicans [are] wannabe gang members. I don't understand that. This is not a bad area. There is nothing bad about this neighborhood. And they just trying to be all tough, and I just look at them and laugh. That's the only thing that makes me mad. All of them think they are tough but they are really not." He added: "The Mexicans dudes, I don't mess with them, 'cause they are just annoying and I end up hurting one of them." When I asked him how he had managed to avoid fighting with them, he replied that being on probation and knowing that he would have to go back to the JTDC made him think twice about beating them up. Probation was thus not an unequivocally negative force in the teenagers' lives. Yet, denied the possibility of accomplishing something through autonomous and creative actions, the teenagers learned to live within the parameters of the system. Success was defined as making it home on time, getting off home confinement, or slowly increasing one's radius of movement.

FEAR AND SELF-LOATHING

Even though the restrictions of probation and parole helped some teenagers to desist temporarily, everyone found the emotional pressure difficult to deal with. José, for example, was tempted to cut off his ankle bracelet and just run away. When he saw on Facebook that his friends were partying, he tried to get the bracelet off with scissors but then stopped. Having an ankle bracelet forced him to stay at his parents' home. He constantly fought with his parents and wondered whether being at the Eliot Detention Center was not a better option for him—at least his parents wouldn't bother him there.

The ankle bracelet made Darell feel claustrophobic, as well. "I am aggravated physically and mentally about school and probation, the curfew. Everything." He admitted that he didn't know how to deal with his feelings. "I just need to relieve my stress. I have nothing to take it out on. I just keep thinking over and over again about the stuff that stresses me out. The bracelet and . . . certain other things. Curfew. The timing." Paradoxically, Darell seemed a lot calmer when he was incarcerated at the Eliot Detention Center. Being on the outside but unable to do what he wanted to do was more challenging for him than being completely removed from his social environment.

Unlike most of the other teenagers, Peter never attempted to rationalize his probation as helpful. In his opinion probation was the cause of his problems. Peter was a thin, dark-skinned African American teenager. He lived with his grandmother and two sisters on Chicago's West Side. Peter was very quiet and I was surprised when he signed up to participate in my research. He was on probation because he had sold marijuana to an undercover policeman. He claimed that he had found a marijuana package on the streets and assumed that someone must have dropped it to avoid getting arrested. He also insisted that this was his first attempt at drug dealing.

Peter explained to me that he had been in juvenile court, but since he was seventeen at the time of his latest arrest, he was assigned to the adult system. During our conversation it was obvious that he had emotional problems. Because of his reclusiveness, it was difficult for him to build trust and open up in conversations. After I met with him for a few weeks, he was sent back to Cook County Jail after receiving too many write-ups in school and attacking a teacher.

When Peter returned to Healy North, he was shaken and even more withdrawn then before. I started the interview by telling him that I was sorry he had been sent back to jail. He just replied, "It was my fault." he understood that he needed help dealing with his anger. He agreed that he should probably talk to someone to learn how to prevent his emotions from boiling over. He just didn't know who to turn to. When I mentioned Peter's case to Healy North's assistant principal, she agreed that Peter needed more support. She was going to send him to a social worker. Peter, however, just wanted to switch schools. "It is too many rules [at Healy North] and then you get wrote up for no reason," he said.

Peter's stay in Cook County Jail, though brief, had thrown him out of balance. Tears welled up in his eyes when I asked him to talk about what it felt like to be incarcerated. He responded quietly: "Days go by slow in there. So you feel like eight days is eight years in there." Peter was consumed by the fear that he would not manage to adhere to the conditions of his probation. The week he had spent in jail was his last chance. His judge had explained to him that he would be sent away for three years if he violated his probation again. He urgently needed to find strategies to cope with his anger. During the week Peter was incarcerated, he had turned to religion. His grandmother was a Jehovah's Witness and Peter began to study the writings of that faith. The Jehovah's Witnesses came by his house on Sundays to teach him.

Peter's offending trajectory was different from that of the other teenagers, but he also instinctively looked for a structural or ideological framework that would make it easier for him to exercise self-control. For Lucas the ankle bracelet was a reminder that he could not recidivate without getting caught. Peter, on the other hand, tried to use a restrictive belief system as the means to control his behavior.

For all the teenagers I interviewed, probation extended their focus on obedience, self-blame, and disconnection from their social environment beyond their incarceration. When I began my research, the young men theoretically had their whole lives ahead of them. Yet some had already, at the age of seventeen, reached a dead end. Regardless of their past or their possible future, the young men wanted to be successful. The artificial structure of parole and probation allowed them to experience success and accomplishment. Embracing and even welcoming their postrelease supervision was not only a rhetorical exercise in meaning-making (Maruna 2001); it also rendered their interactions with a complex environment as the more manageable task of obeying rules and fulfilling clearly structured requirements.

CONCLUSION: SELF-CONTROL AND
SELF-FULFILLMENT

As the teenagers transitioned from juvenile justice facilities to their community, they were put on probation or parole. The level of restriction imposed on them ranged from a few announced visits, in the case of most Chicago teenagers, to constant supervision through ankle bracelets, as in Boston. GPS monitors allowed caseworkers and probation officers to track the teenagers' movement constantly. Being monitored by a GPS device was the ultimate form of control, short of being incarcerated. The teenagers knew that if they were to commit a crime, they would be held accountable. Some were resentful of their continuous supervision. Others embraced the structure of control surrounding them and perceived their supervision as helpful and necessary to ensuring their desistance from crime.

The immediacy of punishment and the experience of tangible rewards for good behavior were core aspects of the young men's rationalizations. The parameters of probation and parole segmented a challenging postin-carceration reality into attainable goals. Because of probation requirements their social world continued to be reduced to obeying the rules that juvenile justice had set up for them. Within this familiar framework, they had the opportunity of feeling a sense of accomplishment.

Nevertheless, the emotional burden on the young men was undeniable. Anxious about violating the parole or probation conditions, the teenagers began to believe that self-control could be achieved only at the expense of self-fulfillment. The teenagers' habitus began to reflect the assumptions that juvenile justice had made about them (Bourdieu 1984; Mead 1969). As a result, the youths' expectations about their quality of life were low as well. They counted themselves lucky that they were still alive and had not been arrested for more serious crimes. As the teenagers rationalized their supervision and confinement, they continued to believe in the promise of an American meritocracy. The young men perpetuated two conflicting narratives about themselves (Leverentz 2014). Although they believed that they could achieve anything if they wanted to, they had given up on being creative actors.

7 "I know how to control myself"

AUTONOMY AND DISCIPLINE IN
THE DESISTANCE PROCESS

When I moved to Boston to set up my second field site, our daughter was almost a year old and my husband had recently started an academic appointment at Wellesley College. Wellesley offered faculty housing, and we decided to settle right on the picturesque campus in a place within walking distance of his office. According to the 2010 census, the median income in Wellesley, Massachusetts, was $155,000. Eighty-five percent of the population was white, 9.8 percent Asian, 3.6 percent Latino, and 2 percent black. I always thought of Wellesley's city center as a quintessential New England town: manicured lawns, white picket fences in front of well-maintained mansions. Young upper-middle-class families move to Wellesley to escape the Boston Public School System and to raise their children in a safe environment.

It usually took me forty-five minutes to drive to Dorchester, the part of Boston where most of the teenagers I interviewed lived. Dorchester symbolizes everything people who move to Wellesley try to escape from: diversity, underperforming schools, and high crime. Actually, Dorchester seemed far more livable than my first field site, the South Side of Chicago. I noticed hardly any empty lots or abandoned buildings and I never heard gunshots. According to the 2010 census 46 percent of Dorchester's population is black and 17 percent are Hispanic or Latino. Yet, on an average summer day, young white families, likely priced out of the heavily gentrified Jamaica Plain, pushed their strollers up Savin Hill Avenue, and UMass Boston students sat in the local frozen yogurt shop to do coursework. The parts of Dorchester I visited did not feel as segregated as Chicago's South Side. At least superficially, there seemed a peaceful coexistence between traditional neighborhood residents, the student population, and newly arriving families. Nevertheless, life in the western suburbs of Boston and the lives of the teenagers I interviewed could not have been more different.[1]

My conversations with other mothers from Wellesley centered on how we could more effectively cultivate our barely two-year-old children (Lareau 2003). Was the early-childhood music class really the best one in town? Did the ballet teacher pay adequate attention to our aspiring dancers? What type of preschool were we going to choose? I wanted my daughter's future identity to be shaped by a diverse set of skills and, more important, all the things she loves to do and succeeds in. As my interviews in Dorchester and Chicago progressed, I came to realize that the youths I met in the study defined themselves mostly through the things they couldn't do—for example, staying out past curfew, going to certain parts of the neighborhood, hanging out with gang-involved friends, taking drugs. Their new, nondeviant identity was not shaped by positive experiences of the self but by successful avoidance of potential reasons for getting arrested again (Leverentz 2014).

The South Side of Chicago is in many ways a more difficult place to grow up in than Dorchester. When I drove past Washington Park on 55th Street in Chicago for the first time, the closest analogy that came to mind was bombed-out German cities after World War II—abandoned and crumbling buildings, empty lots overgrown with grass.[2] Homeless people pushed their belongings down the street in shopping carts. Having grown up in Germany—a welfare state where the government pays for your health insurance, apartment, and cost of living if you are unemployed—I had never seen such poverty before. Some of the teenagers I followed in Chicago struggled with abject poverty. The juvenile justice system in Chicago did not have a centralized caseworker system that could develop individualized reentry plans. It therefore did little to address the youths' difficult living situations. Approximately a third of the teenagers

I followed in Chicago fell through the cracks and ended up in the adult criminal justice system.[3]

Paradoxically, the lack of care also meant that the teenagers in Chicago were far less supervised and controlled than their counterparts in Boston. The teenagers' relative freedom and autonomy were unintended consequences of an overwhelmed juvenile justice system.

CREATIVE VERSUS AUTOMATIC DESISTANCE

Toward the end of his life, Michel Foucault moved away from his interest in how institutional structures generate subordinate subjects and instead began to focus on "Technologies of the Self" (Martin, Huck, and Hutton 1988). In his lectures at the Collège de France, later published as the collection *Hermeneutics of the Subject* (2005), Foucault began to conceptualize a space beyond the structural mechanisms of discipline that allowed the individual to exercise creativity with respect to his identity development. Foucault referred to "taking care of the self" as a technique that begins as an internal process. It is a form of submission to social structures that the self exercises internally and autonomously, supported by disinterested external forces and fundamentally creative in its manifestation. I argue that the concept of taking care of the self clarifies the different forms of desistance the teenagers in Boston and Chicago engaged in.

The Boston teenagers desisted from crime mostly by exercising self-control. The youths mainly aspired to conform to the structural limitations the juvenile justice system imposed on them. This type of conformity is not to be equated with submission to power structures. Many youths cognitively distanced themselves from the programs they were forced to participate in (Scott 1987; E. Goffman 1959). Nevertheless, their desistance process lacked a creative component of self-directed choice about their future. Desistance in Boston was not a transformative experience that expanded the young men's visions of themselves and their futures (Sampson and Laub 2005). Rather, it anchored the desocialized self-image the youths developed while incarcerated, locating that image in the reality of their community. I refer to this type of desistance as "automatic desistance."

The teenagers in Chicago, on the other hand, were able to desist creatively. Without a paternalistic juvenile system trying to make decisions for them, they often followed their own preferences. What I refer to as "creative desistance" takes place outside the instrumental-rational relationships fostered by the juvenile justice system. Creative agency in the desistance process goes beyond the exercise of self-control in the face of power structures. It means connection rather than disconnection from the social environment, and it is the expression of human autonomy. Creative desistance becomes possible when the teenager is able to autonomously employ techniques of the self that may support discipline but are based on pedagogical relationships that the teenager engages in voluntarily. As Foucault (2005) writes, "This work on the self with its attendant austerity is not imposed on the individual by means of civil law or religious obligation, but it is a choice about existence made by the individual. People decide for themselves whether or not to care for themselves" (271).

Differentiating between automatic and creative desistance also allows me to connect the structural interventions of the juvenile justice systems with the identity development of the young men in my study. Conceptually, the structural conditions of the juvenile justice system are set up to prevent the exercise of creative agency. It is only in moments when the system inadvertently allows for the possibility of taking care of one's self beyond exercising self-control that creative desistance can take place.

TEENAGERS' PATHWAYS INTO AND OUT OF CRIME

Trevor, Damon, Jason, and Tyrell faced distinct, complex circumstances when they returned to their neighborhoods. Despite their differences, all of them wanted to become successful adults. They dreamed about going to college, becoming an entrepreneur, or joining the navy; and they professed their willingness to work hard to make it happen. As the four of them struggled to stay away from the streets, their patterns of recidivism and desistance were largely defined by the presence or absence of the juvenile justice system in their lives. As Victor Rios (2011) and others have observed, the more teenagers are supervised and controlled, the more likely it is that they will be caught violating the conditions of their parole or probation (see also Fader 2013; A. Goffman 2014). On the other hand, if they are left without any supervision, falling back into old habits is easy, especially in a moment of crisis. The four cases, described below, exemplify the difference between automatic desistance in Boston and creative desistance in Chicago. They clarify the importance of agency in the desistance process and reveal the limits of the juvenile justice system, as well as the opportunities it offers, to support teenagers in reaching their goal of becoming successful adults.

Trevor

Trevor was sixteen years old when I first met him in the spring of 2010. Unlike most of the children at Healy North, he took the group sessions that the Scholarship and Guidance Association (SGA) offered during the school day seriously. Trevor was a light-skinned, broad-shouldered boy with an athletic build. His brown hair was cut short. He was always friendly and respectful to the social workers in the room. Because of his composed demeanor, I was surprised when he diagnosed himself as having an "anger problem." He was sent to the Saura Center for eight weeks as part of the JDAI. Before coming to the center, he had spent about two weeks in the JTDC.

In one of our sessions at the end of May 2010, he openly shared the nature of his crime. He and two friends were hanging out at a Metra stop on the South Side. His friend suddenly started attacking a college student who was wearing an iPod while waiting for the train. Trevor believed his friend just started the fight because "he thought that we think he is lame. He wanted to show off, because he was usually the one who said that we should not be getting into fights." Trevor joined the fight to "help his friend out." One of his friends grabbed the iPod and they started running. Someone called the police. The three of them were eventually cornered in a back alley and arrested.

When I asked what he wanted to accomplish after his release from the Saura Center, he laid out a rather conventional, middle-class plan for his near future. "My goal is to finish high school. I don't wanna be disrespectful anymore to teachers and my family. I wanna have my own family and be successful. When I get out and back in school, I wanna join a sports team. I am playing all kinds of sports, basketball, football, baseball. I also do track and field. I wanna be successful at sports because I wanna get a scholarship to go to college."

At our last meeting in May 2012, almost two years after our first encounter, Trevor was about to graduate from high school. He was going to start college in Missouri in the fall on a football scholarship. His probation was going to end once his classes had begun. Asked to reflect on what had changed for him over the past two years, he described his desistance as a process of slowing down. "Two years ago . . . I used to get into so much trouble two years ago. And then I just stopped. I won't say I just stopped, but I slowed down to a halt. . . . After I got out, I just didn't wanna get in no more trouble. Some people like being incarcerated. I didn't. I like being outside and free. So I said, 'I don't wanna go back. And I don't wanna do nothing that's gonna put me [back] there.'" This self-reflection only partially captures his transformation. He did indeed "slow down" over the course of two years. Yet the process of desistance I was able to observe was not a linear progression from deviance to desistance. It was rather a roller-coaster ride marked by ups and downs and dependent on fortunate coincidences. Trevor officially recidivated once during the time of my observations, and at least once more, he was on the verge of being returned to the detention center as a result of school suspensions.

HOME LIFE AND NEIGHBORHOOD

In the sample of sixteen Chicago teenagers, Trevor was the only one whose parents were married and lived in the same household. His mother had a master's degree in education. His father was an emergency medical technician. Trevor's mother became pregnant with his older sister while still a teenager, and Trevor's parents got married while both of them were in college. His mother described her marriage has having been difficult at times, "but in the end we always made it work." Trevor's youngest sister was born in May 2010. His immediate neighbors appeared to be middle-class, like his parents. Midsize cars were parked outside mowed, neatly fenced-in lawns. There were no boarded-up houses, abandoned cars, or empty lots full of trash as were common in other more run-down parts of Chicago's South Side. On the other hand, Trevor did not have to go far to reach more dangerous and dilapidated areas (Pattillo-McCoy 1999). The violence regularly spilled over into his neighborhood. Trevor therefore felt it was unsafe to let his sister play outside. He conceded that he would prefer to raise his own children in a more peaceful area.

TEMPORARY DESISTANCE

Trevor was released from the Saura Center at the beginning of the summer in 2010. He was put on home confinement for six weeks. In addition, he had to participate in the Evening Reporting Center program. Every day at 4 P.M. a van picked him up and dropped him off at one of the seven centers operating in Chicago. During our first interview after his release, Trevor was excited to be home. He reported that his daily routine was to sleep in until 10 A.M. and spend the hours between 10 A.M. and 4 P.M. hanging out on the porch. While he was in good spirits immediately after his release, the inertia of home confinement began to wear on him after a few weeks, and he became bored watching TV and staying home all day. The most challenging problem for Trevor was his inability to immerse himself in sports. Trevor tried to join the football team at his old school. The team's coach was eager for him to start practice, but because Trevor had been unable to finish the school year while incarcerated, he was suspended from school and could not join the team for summer training. Despite his frustration he did not breach his home confinement. He was convinced that his probation officer would immediately bring any probation violation in front of his judge. "He [his probation officer] seems like a good guy," Trevor told me. "A cool guy, more or less. But he is serious about his job. . . . If he got to, he would violate me quickly. So I am gonna do what I gotta do." Because of his good behavior Trevor was indeed taken off home confinement at the beginning of August.

RECIDIVISM

Trevor's situation became more challenging after his home confinement came to an end. He was put on probation for two and a half years. The stipulations were to attend school and to avoid associations with gangs and drugs. In addition, he had to do community service and was enrolled in two more JDAI programs. While he was excited about being able to leave the house, the prospect of two and half years on probation made him feel trapped. As a rehabilitative aspect of his probation he was able to continue art therapy, something he had enjoyed during his time at the Saura Center. Unfortunately, playing sports, an important part of his strategy for staying out of trouble, continued to be delayed. For three weekly meetings in a row he expected the problem of reenrollment in his old school to be resolved. His inability to start football training dominated our conversations. The amount of self-confidence he drew from sports was obvious. His coach regularly called to see if he had made any progress on registering at school.

TREVOR: Every time he [his coach] calls he is like, "Why are you not up there?" And I am telling him I am trying to get it together.

M.S.: But that's a good feeling, right, that they really want you to be on the team?

TREVOR: That's a great feeling. They need me.

At the end of August, I called Trevor's mother, as I did every week, to set up an appointment with him. To my surprise she told me, "Trevor is locked up again." She was on her way to a vacation for her wedding anniversary and was extremely upset that Trevor had been misbehaving. He had disappeared after a fight, and Trevor's mother had decided to let his probation officer know that he was not obeying the rules of the house and had left without permission. She explained: "I'd rather have him be locked up than be out on the streets. At least I know where he is. At least I know that he is safe." Trevor was picked up shortly after he returned home and was readmitted to the JTDC. After a week there, Trevor was sent to the Saura Center for another four weeks. Trevor told me that he just went to a friend's house for "a little while." Yet he understood why his mother had called his probation officer. "I got angry for no reason really. So I see why it was caused [readmission to the JTDC]." After a month Trevor returned to his parents. He believed that this time it will be easier to keep his cool: "'Cause now I am not at home all day; I'll be at school so it is less stuff to get agitated about quickly. So it's all right."

Trevor violated his probation at a time when he had nothing to do. He was not in school yet, his probation had just started, and art therapy had not begun yet. Furthermore, he had been unsuccessful in joining the football team. Trevor was keenly aware of how important it was for him to have sports as a way of releasing stress. Right after he started school, he joined the basketball team. During the first few months of the 2010–11 school year, he kept his grades up and stayed away from fights. When I asked him what had changed, he replied, "Before I wasn't worried about the consequences." Trevor continued to fill up his schedule with sports activities. "I need to keep myself busy," he said.

WALKING ON THE EDGE OF RECIDIVISM

In spring 2011, Trevor began to struggle in school again. He received suspension after suspension, mostly for minor infringements like the episode below:

> My mama called my phone when I was in class. My phone went off and the teacher asked for it. She got to yelling and stuff. . . . She said she gave us a warning [that] if it went off, she was gonna take it. She never gave me that warning. 'Cause I wasn't there at the beginning of the school year, so I didn't know. And that was the first time my phone went off in class. She just got to yelling, give it to me, get out and all that stuff. So I am like, "I ain't give you nothing." I just sat there.

By the beginning of April he had collected over sixty days of suspension, and his probation officer warned him that if he had one more suspension in the next thirty days, he would have to go to court for violation of his probation requirements. A week passed and Trevor was again suspended. He had passed a note with death threats from one student to another one. The school considered this the instigation of a fight. Trevor did not understand the severity of his offense. "It ain't the case that I am telling them to fight. He gonna kill you, go beat 'im up and kill him. I am just sayin' watch out. He know where you live. Your mama in this house, your sister. Your grandma. You know, you gonna be on the lookout. But they made it seem like I was gonna say, 'Hey, he gonna try kill you, so you better kill him before he kill you.'" Having been suspended from school for five days, he was preparing himself for spending more time in the JTDC. At the same time, he was still hoping that his suspension might somehow escape the notice of his probation officer. In the end, Trevor did not have to go back to court. He suspected that it was related to paperwork not signed or some other miscommunication.

How another admission to the JTDC would have affected Trevor remains a matter of speculation. It is likely that he would have missed more school and that his grades would have been affected significantly. He might not have been able to enter his senior year of high school. A probation violation would probably also have disrupted the careful balance Trevor had achieved in his life despite his write-ups in school. After the basketball season was over, he joined the baseball team. He was committed to the game and spent several afternoons during the week at practice or at games. He enjoyed art therapy, and in his perspective on the overall trajectory of his life was positive. He pulled his grades from a wintertime downward spiral. He went to school on time, and best of all, he had not committed any more crimes.

SETTLING DOWN

In December 2011 Trevor entered his final year of high school. Asked if he continued to have trouble in school, he replied, "My teacher said that I have been all good and everything. Everything turned around this year." Trevor suspected that it was easier for him to focus on school now because other students respected the fact that he was a senior and that being in school is serious business for seniors. "When people see you, . . . I mean they understand but they don't. They are still tempted [to provoke you], but they not gonna mess around and go fighting and all that stuff, because you are a senior, you got things on the line. In other grades they don't really care." His outlook on the future was unequivocally positive. A small college in Missouri had already contacted him about the possibility of playing football. His coach now had to provide videotapes to finalize the arrangement, but even if his football coach did not come through for him, Trevor was confident that his baseball coach would step up. "My baseball coach, he is gonna look out for me. So I all I gotta do is do my thing in baseball, and then they gonna call some schools and get me a scholarship that way. Either way, I am gonna get something." He looked forward to leaving the South Side of Chicago behind. "A lot of people don't wanna leave. I wanna leave [for Missouri] because it is new. New people. I could start over. . . . You can always come home. It is just being able to go around. And if I can, I want to study abroad." Six months later his future was finalized. He had received the scholarship and was going to play football in

Missouri. He had not run into any major trouble at school, and he commented that having an end in sight made it easier for him ignore distractions. "It's coming to an end [high school]. All the kiddie things are over with. It's stepping up to the real world."

THE ROLE OF AGENCY

Even though probation imposed a structure of control, Trevor was still able to take care of himself in the Foucauldian sense. First, he correctly assessed his ability to excel in sports and relentlessly pursued his desire to be on school teams. He decided not only to play what he loved most, football, but also to join his school's basketball and baseball teams. As a result of his commitment, he was able to generate his coaches' support despite his troubles at school. He also enjoyed his art therapy and took advantage of the opportunity to work introspectively on his transformation. While his attitude toward the streets and his old social environment did initially reflect a desocialized image of self-control, he succeeded in replacing his street life with something meaningful to him. Doing sports boosted his self-esteem. It was not something probation imposed on him, but an activity that he had chosen for himself. Being on the football field, basketball court, or baseball field empowered him to work through his struggles at school, graduate from high school, and win a scholarship. Trevor successfully pursued creative desistance and set the stage for a transformation of his identity that was anchored in his community rather than established in opposition to it.

Trevor was also lucky to have two parents with regular incomes and an overall-stable home environment. In contrast to the other teenagers in Boston and Chicago, Trevor could rely on his parents to be there for him. They advocated for him and, at least initially, made sure that he kept up with his basic probation requirements. Coming from a middle-class family, Trevor did not need the juvenile justice system to provide for his basic needs such as shelter, clothes, and food. When the juvenile system stopped supervising him, he could rely on his familial resources in building an identity defined by more than just complying with probation requirements. Other teenagers in Chicago were not so fortunate as Trevor. Damon's life history, for example, was more representative of the extreme disadvantages that Chicago teenagers had to cope with as they tried to "go straight."

Damon

I met Damon for the first time in October 2009 when he had just turned eighteen. I had only a vague idea of what my dissertation project might look like when I started visiting a youth center run by the Catholic Precious Blood order on the South Side of Chicago. Damon was part of a core group of youths who had been coming there since their early teens. Every Wednesday at 5:30 P.M., Father David Kelly, who ran the center, invited neighborhood boys to join a peace circle and to reflect on a set of prepared questions. A talking piece was passed around. Every teenager was allowed to say what was on his mind, but he was also free to pass the piece on if he did not feel like sharing any thoughts. The questions often related to the young men's daily struggles, but Father Kelly also encouraged them to think about the positive moments in their lives.

Damon participated in these circles almost every week. Before the circle started, he was usually hanging out with his friends. They would be joking around, laughing, playing pool or computer games. Damon did not share his thoughts often during the circles, but he listened to others and was sincere about participating most of the time. He had a great sense of humor, and his dry sarcasm reminded me of the comedian Patrice O'Neal. With hair cut short, he was tall and had a rather small build. When he officially enrolled in my study, in June 2010, he also had a concrete plan for his future. He wanted to visit the places where he had lived before moving to Chicago, then join the navy. "As soon as I graduate, I am gonna go to Iowa. I graduate like four months before I walk across the stage, so I am gonna go to Iowa until the week that I am gonna walk across the stage. Then come back, lunch and prom and all of that, walk across the stage. Then after that I wanna go to Memphis . . . and then to the navy from Memphis."

But, unlike Trevor, who reached the goals he had set for himself, Damon did not graduate from high school. His dream of leaving the streets behind and leading a predictable middle-class life shattered when he was arrested at the end of August 2010 and eventually convicted of armed robbery. He was released in 2013 after serving three years of a five-year sentence at a maximum-security prison in Illinois. With a felony on his record, he was not able to join the navy.

HOME LIFE AND NEIGHBORHOOD

Damon's family life was very unstable. Damon's family was originally from Chicago. His mother had nine children and lost custody of all of them except the youngest. He and his younger sister were adopted by the same family, but Damon never settled into that family. His adoptive mother kicked him out when he continued to be arrested. In his early teens, Damon moved to live with his brother in Iowa, where he was sent to juvenile prison for over a year. After his release, he decided to go back to Chicago. When I met him in the fall of 2009, he was living with his biological mother on the far South Side of Chicago. He later explained to me that after his final arrest, his juvenile judge had allowed him to move back in with his birth mother, even though she had lost her maternal rights long ago. In the fall of 2009 Damon became a father himself. He and his girlfriend had an on-again, off-again relationship, but eventually broke up soon after the baby boy was born. Damon's son continued to spend time at Damon's mother's house with his little cousins. Damon, his mother, and his sister took turns babysitting. He spent a lot of his free time at the Precious Blood Center. He used the computer, was able to get free food, and was also paid for participating in art projects. It was the Precious Blood Center—Father Kelly in particular—not his family, that anchored him in Chicago. In July 2010 he told me, "Ain't really a lot here in Chicago. The only reason I stay in Chicago is for the center. That's it."

Damon was enmeshed in the violence of the neighborhood that surrounded the center, which was located in the heart of Englewood. Several friends of his had been shot at in the area. He was afraid that the same thing could happen to him. Though not a gang member, he would hang out outside with his friends, gambling and smoking weed, and he was aware that whatever trouble caused his friends to be attacked could potentially harm him as well. "Ryan got shot. That was the first day of the summer. . . . Like he had just got out of school two hours ago. Then after that, two weeks later Mad Man [another friend] got shot. Then I am like, 'Aha, the dude that shot Mad Man, he mad at me too. He wanna shoot me.'"

TEMPORARY DESISTANCE

By July 2010 Damon's mother had moved from the South Side to Evanston, Illinois. Damon was able to move in with his sister. She had moved into independent living, and her apartment was paid for by DCFS. She lived in a fairly quiet area, close to the South Shore neighborhood. Damon's plan was to lay low over the summer. "I am just gonna stay in the house. Just do me. Keep on the right track. That is the only thing that's gonna stop me; if I get killed, get shot that's gonna mess up my life." Having spent half a year at the alternative school located below the Precious Blood Center, he was confident that this upcoming high school year was going to be his last. Over the summer he was getting paid to work at a mural project organized by Father Kelly. Although he admitted that the most intriguing part of the mural project was getting paid, he was proud of the artwork. "People we know walk past and they are, 'Hey, you all paint this? Good job, good job. It is you all painting that down there? You are doing good.' So we are all getting a lot of compliments down there." Since his release from juvenile prison in Iowa, he had been arrested once for breaking and entering and theft in Chicago. He had spent time at the Juvenile Detention Center and the Saura Center. Yet, between the time I met him in October 2009 and our first official interview in July 2010, he had not been in the JTDC again. His living situation seemed to have stabilized, and he even enjoyed going to school. When I asked him in mid-August how his schoolwork was going, he replied: "Good. I was talking more to the females there and I have been doing all my work. So I have been having fun and still doing my work."

RECIDIVISM

Less than two weeks later, by the end of August, Damon's life turned upside down. His sister threw him out of her apartment. She and her boyfriend claimed he had stolen $500. Damon denied the accusations. "That's a lot of money too. Five hundred dollars. I mean at least if I had stolen something, it would have probably taken ten dollars, out of five hundred, something like that instead of the whole five hundred." He thought that his sister's boyfriend wanted to get rid of him because he was not paying rent or providing them with anything else useful. He speculated, "I was supposed to get a food stamp card. I bet if I had that [or] something like that I would be still living there." He was shocked that his sister would kick him out so suddenly:

> [The] only thing I want is to stay over at [my sister's] crib until I graduate. You supposed to let somebody do that. A person that go to school! Messin' with somebody who go to school! You never supposed to do that! . . . You don't do your family like that. You supposed to be nice. After all that stuff we have been through you . . . should never do anything like that to your brothers and sisters.

During our conversation we discussed various housing options. He could not live with his father, because his father did not have a place to stay, either. His girlfriend had recently been thrown him out of her apartment. His mother's new place was a suboptimal solution as well. To take public transportation from Evanston, at the opposite end of the city, to his school would have taken him at least an hour and a half. Moreover, he felt it was wrong to impose on his mother. She had just moved in with a new boyfriend, he said, and "she met this dude who got money. His wife died so she moved there [to Evanston] with him. So I am like, that's good. It is about time that she got somebody, you know, that can support her. 'Cause she just be working, all the other boyfriends didn't even go to work. They just be drinking. So I am like, I ain't wanna mess with that [this mother's new relationship]. You are doing good." Father Kelly could not help him because he already had another young man staying with him. When I finally suggested that maybe he could return to his adoptive mother, he replied, "She kicked me out. She said I can't come back." He had a friend that he could stay with for a week, but that was not a permanent solution. He felt that fate had turned against him. "Ever since school started back up, I was doing good. Good in school. Liking the females, females liking me. Going home, game playing. Everything [was] good. And then that shit. Getting kicked out. Now school doesn't even feel so good no more. I don't feel right at school." He was embarrassed that his sister had kicked him out and frustrated over what he felt was a false accusation. "I almost wish I did stole some stuff, man. I never have, but I wish I did. At least I would have had something."

Less than a week after our meeting, Damon did try to take something. He robbed a man using a BB gun. When I visited Damon in Cook County Jail a month later, he explained that he had not been thinking before the robbery. He admitted that it was the stupidest thing he had ever done. He claimed that he did not even get anything out of it, because the man was broke. The man identified Damon a day after the robbery. Damon was sitting on a porch, and the man he had robbed passed by, recognized him, and called the police. Damon caught a break when he was sent to a four-month boot camp in spring 2011. His graduation was scheduled for that summer, but after he got into a fight with his cellmate, he was sent to a medium-security prison where I visited him in December 2011. He was upbeat and had a positive outlook. He was studying for his GED and earning what is referred to as good time, meaning that the time he was spending in the GED program would be deducted from his sentence. He expected to be out by June 2012.

In February 2012 Damon was transferred to a maximum-security prison. He had allegedly pushed a guard. In addition to being relocated to a different facility, he also lost the good time he had earned. Damon sent the only letter he was allowed to write to the Precious Blood Center. He planned to spend the time until his parole date in June 2013 watching TV in his cell. His goal was to minimize interactions with guards or other inmates.

THE ROLE OF AGENCY

In Damon's case the juvenile justice system in Chicago was conspicuously absent. The lack of a punitive framework allowed Damon to establish a network of support at the Precious Blood Center that was of his own making. Initially he was able to take care of himself as he built noninstrumental relationships that supported his identity transformation. He joined the weekly peace circles voluntarily, a forum that allowed him to engage in introspective reflection. With the help of Father Kelly he was able to enroll in an alternative school. Nevertheless, over the summer, Damon also expressed a desocialized vision of his desistance. He wanted to stay inside and play computer games in his free time. He was fortunate, though, that the majority of his day was taken up with Kelly working on a mural. Disconnecting from the street, therefore, did not leave him without a social life. Being at the center allowed him to engage with peers without the risks involved in being on the corner. Damon did undoubtedly engage in creative desistance. Unfortunately, his creative agency hit a limit when he became homeless. Being left without a place to stay exposed his vulnerability and upset the balance of the routines he had set up for himself. Because he was still in high school and did not have the resources to rent an apartment or even a room, what agency he had was severely confined by structural boundaries. Getting kicked out of his sister's apartment made him hopeless. All the hard work of taking care of himself seemed meaningless in the face of this insurmountable obstacle. He again exercised agency when he robbed someone. Yet the choice he made was framed by adverse structural circumstances.

It is safe to say that Damon would have probably fared very differently in the Boston juvenile justice system. Massachusetts's tightly organized juvenile probation and parole structures the teenagers' lives on the outside. In my experience, if teenagers hit a rough spot, the DYS provided basic support such as shelter, food, and family therapy. At the same time, as Jason's example below shows, the teenagers lacked the ability to desist from crime on their own terms. Their identity development was constrained by the structural boundaries juvenile justice had established around their lives.

Jason

In the late summer of 2011, just a few weeks short of turning seventeen, Jason was arrested for carrying a gun. After several months at the Eliot Detention Center in Dorchester, Massachusetts, he was committed to the DYS and sent from the detention unit to an assessment unit, where he stayed for approximately one month. He was finally placed in what the DYS referred to as a nonsecure treatment center, where he remained for six more months.

Jason had long braided hair. Tall, broad shouldered, and light skinned, he was very quiet, almost withdrawn, and he behaved impeccably at every facility he was sent to.[4] When he was arrested, Jason was on his way to a memorial service for his cousin, who had been shot a few days earlier. He was very close to this cousin. "I hate to even think about it. He is more like my brother, though. I have seen him almost every day." Jason was walking with a group of friends to the service when one of them asked him to hold on to a gun. Jason claimed that he was not planning to use the weapon.

"We were walking on Blue Hill Avenue. The detectives pulled up, and then they got out of the car. Then I walked away from the group slowly and then I started to run. About two minutes later they handcuffed me and I was arrested."

FAMILY LIFE AND NEIGHBORHOOD

Jason lived with his parents and brothers—one younger, the other older—in Dorchester. His mother also took care of her daughter's two young children while Jason's sister was working and finishing college. Jason's father was struggling with alcoholism. "He has a drinking problem," Jason said. "He is not abusive, though. When he comes home, he is more like, 'Roar roar roar,' like mad loud." Jason was sick of seeing his father in this state and happy that he decided to go to rehab while Jason was incarcerated. His father had been to rehab before, but Jason was still optimistic that he would stick with it this time. Despite his father's struggles, he was glad that his parents had not gotten a divorce. "I am happy that they are still together. It is not [the case] that I don't love my dad because he has bad habits." Jason used to smoke weed every day, a habit that he was forced to break while incarcerated. He hoped not to pick it up again after his release. "There is no fun in it. It's just you are continually smoking and drinking, and you don't really care what's going on. And your mind is just full of mad emotions. Especially anger. You always want revenge for some odd reason." Jason was also a gang member. He joined after his brother's stabbing made him fear that he was going to get attacked as well. At the same time, he said that he did not admire any of his fellow gang members. He had just joined for protection. Jason clearly perceived his neighborhood as dangerous. Asked why he would not go to the police for protection, he replied that cops didn't about what is going in the neighborhood. "They are there to make money. That is how I look at it. Their job is to fight [crime], but they don't really care what's going on. They are just, you know, making sure they support their family."

One important influence that drew Jason away from his gang activity was his girlfriend. They celebrated their three-year anniversary in the summer of 2012. Although they were fighting a lot and broke up at least once while he was incarcerated, they were back together when Jason was released. Jason claimed she was "crazy" and wanted his attention all the time. He also acknowledged, though, that his girlfriend and her family were a positive influence on him. She disapproved of his gang membership and instead wanted him to spend more time with her. After his release from the treatment center, Jason was not allowed to go home. His brother had been arrested for battery and sent to adult jail. His family lived in Section 8 housing, and one of the requirements to remain was a clean criminal record. Since his brother's name was on the lease, his family was in danger of losing their apartment. Jason's caseworker, therefore, decided to put him temporarily in a foster home. A foster home, she believed, would provide more stability until the family's housing situation was resolved. When I visited him at his foster home, I was overwhelmed by the chaos. The apartment was stuffy and overheated. A huge pile of pots and pans stood in the corner of the dining room. friendly, laid-back elderly African American woman who rant the foster home she seemed not to care very much about the cleanliness of the place. The many fake flowers on top of cabinets and tables were covered with dust. The floor was so dirty that I would not have felt comfortable taking off my shoes. Six teenagers, including Jason, lived in the three-bedroom apartment, the exact opposite of his home. Jason's family had a clean, spacious, and clutter-free place. Jason seemed to have resigned himself to the fact that he had to remain in the foster home for the time being. "It's fine," he said. "It is not like being home, though."

DESISTANCE

When Jason was caught with a gun, he was already on juvenile probation. After he was charged with gun possession, the full punitive force of the Massachusetts juvenile justice system came down on him. He spent almost eight months locked up in DYS facilities. Jason seemed to adjust well to being incarcerated. His good behavior on the assessment unit earned him a spot in a nonsecure treatment center. Although he was not allowed to leave, the setting was more like a group home, comparable to the Saura Center in Chicago, than an adult prison. When he arrived at the treatment center, he kept up his good behavior. While his fellow inmates got into fights, he remained in his room and "stayed out of it." He did not enjoy associating with the other young men and considered them immature. "Everybody kind of has the same mind-set. They just act like little kids. That kind of annoys me. My main goal is just to keep myself focused. My main goal is just get myself out of here, at the end of the day." Jason's imagined desistance was desocialized, driven mainly by the question of how he could avoid not only friends but also family who were still active gang members. "It's easy to stay away from them but then it's not because they are family. When they go out and party and whatever, that is when I need to separate myself. At family reunions, that will be the only time I be actually hanging with them." Initially he had thought of playing basketball as a way of filling the time he had once spent with his gang-member friends. Yet, as his time at the DYS progressed and his caseworker took over, basketball was pushed into the background.

After his release, Jason mostly adhered to the rigorous structure his caseworker established for him. His caseworker had arranged for a job that filled his afternoons. Together with other youths he was painting a warehouse for three hours every day, making $6 per hour. In addition he had to see a therapist once a week. His curfew was 8:00 P.M. on weekdays and 9:00 P.M. on weekends. After school and work and using public transportation to get around, he usually arrived at his foster home around 7:30. His foster mother told me that Jason was never late. He attended school every day, went to work every day, and saw his therapist once a week. On the weekends he was allowed to spend Saturdays with his family but had to be back by curfew. None of the activities he engaged in was something he had chosen for himself. The types of school, work, and therapy in which he was involved were chosen by his caseworker with the main purpose of keeping him so busy that he would not have time to reconnect with his old gang friends. His caseworker encouraged a strategy of avoidance. "She [the caseworker] said to just stay focused on school. . . . Avoiding [trouble]." For the first four weeks he also had to wear an ankle bracelet.

Of all his responsibilities, he enjoyed the job most. "[The job] occupies my time. I am just focusing on me when I am at work. It's a good feeling. And I am getting my own money." His regular attendance in school paid off: he had received an A in history, as he proudly showed me on his transcript. Even though he was doing well and obeying the rules, he seemed unsure as to what extent the time at the DYS had actually transformed the way he acted in relation to his familiar social environment. "How do I act differently? That's a mighty good question. I don't know, 'cause I have just been going to work, going to school, and going to my house and I haven't really been out nowhere." Intensive postincarceration supervision re-created as closely as possible the artificial situation of incarceration. Jason did not have the opportunity to immerse himself in his old neighborhood. He had already excelled in disciplining himself while incarcerated; after his release, he used the same persistence in the face of control and restriction to slowly receive more freedom as a reward for his good behavior. After five months on the outside, Jason had not recidivated. He continued to practice automatic obedience and put into practice the desocialization that he had rehearsed during his incarceration.

THE ROLE OF AGENCY

Jason's ability to act autonomously on the outside was extremely confined. To stay out of trouble, he had to engage in automatic desistance. His schedule was dominated by tasks his caseworker had picked for him. He was not able to find time to play basketball, something he genuinely enjoyed and was successful with. The time he could spend with his girlfriend was also severely limited because she was not allowed to come to the foster home where he lived. Jason could see her only on Saturdays, when he stayed at his parents' house for a few hours. He submitted completely to the rules, hoping that practicing automatic desistance and docility would gradually allow him to regain creative agency. Although he did stay out of trouble for a significant amount of time after he was released, desistance was achieved within a rigorous framework of an almost completely controlled environment. Jason was, without a doubt, extraordinarily resilient, and he successfully adapted to the rigorous schedule the DYS set up for him. Other teenagers struggled to keep up with their requirements and were less adept at upholding their aspirations for upward mobility. Tyrell, for instance, was unable to handle the inevitable frustrations that arose while he tried to keep up with his demanding postrelease schedule.

Tyrell

Tyrell was fifteen in the fall of 2011 when he was arrested for stealing a laptop. Like Jason, he was on juvenile probation, and his judge had committed him to a treatment facility. Tyrell spent two months in the Eliot Detention

Center and another month in the assessment unit. He was placed at a treatment center other than Eliot, located an hour and a half from Boston. Like Jason, he maintained very good behavior in all the units he passed through. He was a tall, almost skinny young man—so tall that he looked older than his age. His treatment center was in a rural setting at the edge of a forest. One of his clinicians mentioned that he was a very needy child. I did not experience him as needy but I had the impression that he was sensitive and looked to adults around him for guidance. He enjoyed the fact that I engaged with him and listened to what he had to say in our interviews. He was very open. His personality was generally gregarious and friendly.

Stealing the laptop, though, was an outcome that indicated a deep involvement in street life. "I owed my friend money. I was selling drugs for my friend but I came short. I spent some of the money so I owed him some. He saw a laptop sitting in the window and he told me, 'If you get me that laptop we are even.' So I grabbed the laptop, and two hours later I got arrested." The owner of the laptop had seen who had taken it and called the police.

HOME LIFE AND NEIGHBORHOOD

Tyrell had grown up in South Boston. A few years before we met, his family had moved to Dorchester. South Boston was also the neighborhood he traveled to in order to sell drugs. He spent the money made from drug dealing mostly on himself, buying marijuana or clothes, and on his girlfriends. Sometimes he would give his mother $120 as "gas money" or so that she could buy herself new clothing. He was never arrested for drug dealing. He said that he started selling drugs because he grew up around it. "I saw the older guys make that much money; why can't I?" Dealing drugs, as he had experienced it, was a dangerous, all-encompassing, and ethically dubious business:

> You could sell to the wrong people. Someone could get out a gun. The people who buy from us, we call them cokeheads, fiends, weedheads. Some drug dealers treat them badly, but I always treat them well. They come begging. If they are short, I will give it to them anyway, but I tell them that they can't come short next time. They need to learn not to come short. I am not treating them bad. If they really need it, I'll give it to them. It is crazy sometimes and it is definitely a lot of work. They even call me at home. I am selling the stuff two train stops from home.

Tyrell had four siblings and every one of them except two had a different father. He was the second youngest. His older sister had been more "like a second mother" to him when he was little. "My mom used to go out and stuff. My sister always used to take care of me." His oldest brother, who was adopted, was in prison for life. He had stabbed a person at a party six years before. Tyrell recalled the night that his brother came home covered in blood: "He came to the house all drunk and bloody. He said, 'I stabbed somebody and I hope he is dead.' Turns out he *was* dead, and the next day the police came to the house and got him." His brother had a history of violence that Tyrell had witnessed before. "I have seen him stab a Mexican dude at a little get-together outside the projects. . . . It was a little baby shower. I was like seven years old. He got into this argument with this drunk dude. He [his brother] wasn't drunk at all. Drunk dude cracked the bottle. He tried to stab him with the cracked bottle, then my brother pulled out the knife and stabbed him in his arm two times." His older brother's incarceration nevertheless came as a shock to Tyrell, and he perceived it as watershed moment for his family. "Ever since my oldest brother got locked up for life, everything changed. One brother joining the gang. My other brother just started being worse. Me, I just started doing stupid stuff. Hanging out, smoking weed with my friends."

His family lived in a three-bedroom apartment. Tyrell, his mother, his two brothers, and his mother's boyfriend lived there permanently. In addition, at one point a couple stayed with them for a few months, and another friend of the family stayed on and off as well. When Tyrell returned home, he did not have a room. Instead he was sleeping on the folded-out living room couch. It did not seem to bother him much. He emphasized the advantage of having the TV in his room. He did not have a desk where he could do homework and said that he could do it anywhere in the house. The apartment was very clean.

His mother, who was warm and welcoming, was always busy driving her family back and forth, going to court for them, and helping out friends who had smaller children. Every two weeks she took care of her one-year-old grandchild. Tyrell's mother was frank about the grief Tyrell and his brothers had caused her. When she met my daughter, she assured me that girls are a lot easier to raise than boys. She had formerly worked as a caretaker for elderly people but had stopped working to focus more on her boys, who were obviously struggling. Tyrell expressed disappointment about his father's absence in his life: "I can't trust my father anymore, though. He is in and out of my life." But when Tyrell was released, he proudly told me that his father had taken him shopping. Overall, Tyrell's family life seemed turbulent. His mother did not have a lot of time to devote to each individual child, but she did what she thought was the best she could do to encourage her children to stay out of trouble. Tyrell also had girlfriends. He stayed in touch with one of them while he was incarcerated, but the relationship seemed to dissolve after he returned to the community. He always had a girl whom he was interested in or dating, but they changed over time.

RECIDIVISM

Although Tyrell did not initially talk to the DYS clinicians about his drug dealing, he did open up to them in the end. While he was still incarcerated, he came to the conclusion that dealing drugs just was not for him anymore. "It's not me, because like I know I could be better in life. I have a lot of support in life. My mom, my mentor, I got a lot of people that support me. Family that supports me. Is no reason why I should be doing all the stuff I did. I could be doing better things. And find out other ways to make money, like getting a job." Instead of dealing, he was thinking of finding a way to work with children and making money in legal ways. "I used to babysit a lot; that got me amped up about working with kids a lot. I don't know. There is just something about kids. . . . I have high energy with kids. It's like I am a kid again. Like playing with them, just little stuff like that." In our first interview after he had returned to his family, Tyrell was excited about being home and seemed positive about the requirements of his probation. Tyrell's caseworker had worked out a fairly strict regimen for him. For the first thirty days he had to be home by 7 P.M. He had to check in with his caseworker every day at that time and had to meet with her three times a week. The DYS also set him up with a mandatory therapist. Regular school attendance was required, as well as going to a job his caseworker would help him find. As time went by, if he did well, curfew and check-ins would be loosened.

About eight weeks after his release, his struggle to adhere to probation requirements became obvious. Keeping up with probation was challenging not only for him but also for his mother, who had to drop him off at various DYS meetings that kept being added to his schedule. "There are so many people in Tyrell's life. It gets confusing. And they want me to do stuff as well," his mother complained. She had apparently missed one of his Friday-afternoon DYS appointments and had remembered only when someone called her and asked about Tyrell's absence. She also believed the DYS was overwhelming Tyrell. "It is a bit too much that they want him to do. Not just for him but for any child. He has school, he has physical therapy, he has to go to meetings on Friday, he is going to work, and then he meets with his street worker, and now he has a new clinician." The Friday DYS meetings also conflicted with the job he had just started. He was participating in a clothing design project his street worker had set him up with. He was excited to be part of this group of young people, who were supposed to learn how to start a business. "I am glad I got this job," Tyrell said. "That's what I wanted. That's what I have been looking for. The clothing design job—I didn't know that it was gonna be like this. I thought I was gonna follow another person's commands, but now I know that people are gonna be following my commands." He also conceded that part of his stress was a price he had to pay for his mistakes. "You know what I think it is: I never had that much pressure on me before. That's why I am really like this. I don't know. I think I am just overreacting. . . . Oh, it is just so much people, but I think . . . I don't know. I never felt this much pressure before, that's why it is like this. But when you grow up, it's gonna be like that sometimes. I didn't do things right; that's what happens."

About two months after he returned home, Tyrell was sent to a revocation unit for violation of parole. When I met him the day after he returned home again, he was embarrassed to talk about what had happened. I had never seen Tyrell as beaten down and depressed as he was that day. His answers, usually voluble, were now terse:

M.S.: So tell me what happened? Where were you?

TYRELL: I got locked up 'cause of school and curfew and I need to do better in grades.

M.S.: How did that happen with your curfew?

TYRELL: Didn't call for a few days. I was here, though, but I didn't call. Plus, most of the time, it was after work and I just didn't call.

M.S.: Why did you not call?

TYRELL: I don't know.

M.S.: You forgot about it?

TYRELL: I guess.

During our conversation he also admitted that he had not shown up to the job that he was originally so excited about. As a result, the other group members decided that he was unreliable and voted him out of the group. He also struggled in school. "And my grades. . . . It was just my grades and . . . I was supposed to stay for detention and I didn't do it. I didn't stay for detention. I left. The next day I was supposed to stay after school. I didn't stay after school; I just left at dismissal time. And they suspended me." He also admitted that he had never done his homework on time. Clearly upset at a situation that he saw as his own fault, he tried to think of other options, such as Job Corps, that could get him out of his home environment. "[I am] getting too much [of] Boston. It's a too small world, too small world. And half of that world is killing each other. I am not trying to be in the Boston world no more. . . . Job Corps would be perfect." His caseworker's advice as to how to avoid further probation violation was simple. As Tyrell recalled, "She just talked to me, just to do better. That's all she wants from me. If you do better, I'll be less hard on you. All that type of stuff." The solution for him was to become more obedient. "You know they try to show me discipline. How to handle myself. I just don't follow through with it. All I need to do is follow through with it and I'll be straight. I was at first, . . . but . . ."

THE ROLE OF AGENCY

Like Jason, Tyrell was supposed to follow rules and keep up with his obligations. Yet Tyrell quickly felt overwhelmed. Over time it became increasingly difficult for him to keep up with his parole requirements. When he made independent choices, such as spending time with his friends, he immediately infringed on DYS rules. Tyrell could express agency creatively only when he already knew that he was going to be sent to a revocation unit. At this point he prioritized short-term freedom over long-term automatic desistance. His mother called him at school to tell him that a warrant was out for his arrest. Jason then decided to spend the weekend at his friend's house, completely free of any DYS obligations. He turned himself in on Monday, as he had promised his mother to do.

CONCLUSION: AUTONOMY AND INEQUALITY

Comparison of the four cases shows that the teenagers' desistance was shaped by the structural contingencies of the juvenile justice system. In Chicago, Damon's recidivism was defined by a lack of structural support. In Boston, Tyrell recidivated because he was unable to cope with the DYS's structural requirements. The creative agency he expressed translated into recidivism. In contrast, Trevor's desistance in Chicago was an autonomous act. The lack of supervision in combination with his parents' support allowed him to exercise creative desistance and to build a network that helped him to achieve the goals he had set for himself. In a Foucauldian sense, he had transcended the power structures of the juvenile justice system and was able to take care of himself. Jason, on the other hand, had to resort to automatic desistance. He implemented the absolute obedience he envisioned during his incarceration. His transformation was successful in terms of the structural framework of the juvenile justice system, but he was not able to take care of himself in a way that allowed him to reengage with his social environment on his own terms.

The juvenile justice system in place at the beginning of the twentieth century has been described as an institution that disciplined and stigmatized working-class children (Platt 1977; Zimring 2005). While it may be too simplistic to equate today's juvenile justice practitioners with the child-savers, parallels are undeniable. Massachusetts's attempt to manage every aspect of the teenagers' lives resonates with Platt's observation (1977) that the early juvenile courts treated adolescents "as though they were naturally dependent, requiring constant and pervasive supervision" (4). Enabling young men to become autonomous actors remains particularly difficult for a juvenile justice system that continues to be based on control and punishment. The young men in Boston and Chicago wanted to live free and fulfilled lives. They lost this privilege, some may argue, when they committed crimes. At the same time, the ability to make independent choices about one's future is considered one of the most important aspects of sustaining desistance in the long term (Gadd and Farrall 2004; Farrall 2005; Sampson and Laub 2005; Vaughan 2007; Carlsson 2012). Thus, if we are truly interested in reducing juvenile recidivism, we have to take the youths' desire for autonomy seriously.

Middle-class and upper-middle-class parents carefully craft their children's identity from early childhood on. Teaching children what they are good at and encouraging them to make choices accordingly has been part of middle class parenting for a long time (Lareau 2003). Fostering talents translates into self-confidence. It enables children to build further skills, and eventually opens doors to elite education and successful careers (Khan 2011). Like other teenagers I followed, Damon, Tyrell, Jason and Trevor believed in the American promise of meritocracy and possibility. Yet their criminal history as well as their social disadvantages often excluded them from making choices and understanding their strengths and weaknesses. Acknowledging the teenagers' longing for living self-actualized lives rather than just getting by at the bottom of the social hierarchy is necessary if we want to seriously address the inequality that mass incarceration and poverty have create in this country (Western 2006).

Conclusion

Dan dreamed about leaving the South Side of Chicago, but even more than that, he envisioned his triumphant return. He imagined how his relatives were going to be surprised that the struggling teenager they knew before had become somebody. Dan wanted to be a psychiatrist. He was articulate and a good listener. Someone had told him that Arizona State University (ASU) had a good psychology program, and that's where we wanted to go. Dan's life had been anything but stable so far. He had moved from place to place, had stayed with different relatives, and finally ended up at the Saura Center after he had assaulted his mother's boyfriend. Dan remained at the Saura Center for months without anywhere to go. Eventually, his great-aunt decided to take him in. Dan felt lucky to finally have a home again, but he continued to be afraid that it was only a temporary placement. His mother did not want him to move back in. If his great-aunt forced him to leave, he would have to live in a group home again.

Although Dan lived fairly close to Hyde Park, he had never been there. My husband and I took him out for lunch and showed him President Obama's Chicago residence. Dan looked like an ordinary college freshman. I could easily picture him on a college campus. He talked a lot about how much he valued education and how urgently he wanted to leave for college. When I left the South Side to move to Boston in 2012, he told me that he would be studying hard over the summer. He knew that he needed to improve his grades and his ACT scores if he wanted to enroll in a four-year college. In December of that year, when I returned for another round of meetings, I asked him how school was going. He admitted that he had given up on studying: "I get lazy. I want to do things, but then it's just hard and I just get tired of it."

Dan struggled because he was not used to overcoming obstacles by engaging with his problems. At the Saura Center he had learned that disconnecting emotionally was the fastest way to achieving his goals. If he wanted to move back into his community, he had to keep quiet, even if he perceived a situation as unfair. He distanced himself from the daily routine of the center: "When they tell you to sit down, you have to sit down. . . . It made me so mad but I had to keep it down, because if I didn't they were gonna book me," he explained. Dan made it through his time at the Saura Center by keeping his head down and focusing on his release (Fader 2013). When he started living with his aunt, he had to do exactly the opposite: to engage with his environment and act strategically in terms of the future that he wanted to build.

Dan had several strikes against him. His high school was one of the worst in the city. According to data provided by the Chicago public school system, 94 percent of the students were low-income. The average ACT score was 14, and only 6 percent of the students who graduated in 2010 enrolled in a four-year college. He also lived in a resource-poor area. He did not have a stable home environment, and his education had been interrupted because of his juvenile justice involvement. Dan also lacked familial resources that could have fostered his curiosity and directed his energy into after-school activities. Even if he studied hard, embarking on a successful professional career would have been difficult for him. Unlike most of the other teenagers I interviewed, he theoretically understood what he needed to do to be upwardly mobile. Yet he lacked a middle-class habitus that would have enabled him to overcome his life's structural boundaries (Lareau 2003; Bourdieu 1984).

The skills he learned while he was at the Saura Center helped him to get off probation without recidivating. His ability to disconnect once a challenging situation arose, however, became detrimental when he needed to work through obstacles at school. He told me that nobody in his family ever studied. It was hard for him to stay in the house when everybody around him was outside having fun. Dan did not know how to prioritize the process of studying, as distinguished from just imagining his future as a college student. Dan finished high school but he never went to ASU. His grades and ACT score were too low to apply to a well-respected school. He even dropped out of Western Illinois University. Dan did not return to the South Side as a success. Five years after we first met, he had desisted from crime, but he still struggled to build a life for himself. Dan's trajectory demonstrates the myriad ways in which juvenile delinquency and inequality overlap and reinforce each other (Piquero and Sealock 2010; Wu, Cernovich, and Dunn 1997; Sampson and Laub 1993). The teenagers' struggles did not end once they had officially left the juvenile justice system. Even though Dan desisted, he was still far from becoming the person he had envisioned.

The young men utilized the narrative of the "American Dream" to redeem themselves (Maruna 2001). Incarceration, in particular, was constructed as a turning point after which a better future could be imagined. The narrative also provided hope when the teenagers had nothing else to hold on to. The myth of American meritocracy obscured racial discrimination and cumulative disadvantage. Unaware of the historical and structural forces that contributed to their marginalization, the teenagers took a highly individualistic approach to explaining their recidivism. They blamed themselves for making "bad choices," for not "listening" to the adults in their lives, or for being "stupid." Their imagined desistance was outcome-oriented and contained unrealistic expectations of radical change. The actual process of desistance was a complex interplay between structural limitations and agentic moves— an ongoing process interspersed with periods of recidivism (Leverentz 2014; Maruna 2001). The young men were often unable to anticipate setbacks. In many cases, they could not conceptualize engaging positively with their social environment. Instead they emphasized their need to restrain themselves and to limit their exposure to their neighborhood and old friends. Distinguishing between automatic and creative desistance acknowledges that desistance is more than temporary nondeviance. It takes into account the fact that creativity and making choices are important parts of constructing a viable nondeviant self. A teenager's success within the structure of juvenile justice does not necessarily mean that he has desisted from crime. He has mostly learned to obey specific rules strategically for a limited amount of time (Reich 2010).

According to Shadd Maruna (2001), optimistic redemption scripts are important for long-term desistance. Rewarding good behavior and providing opportunities to put the desired nondeviant self into practice should therefore be integrated into offender rehabilitation. With the implementation of cognitive behavioral therapy the juvenile justice system has de facto put into practice Maruna's proposal of an "honor roll" for inmates (163). The teenagers in Boston and Chicago received constant affirmation for obeying the rules while they were held in juvenile justice facilities. Yet these experiences did not translate to the outside world. Most of them had never been successful outside the juvenile justice setting. After their release they still lacked the opportunity to experience a nondeviant self in autonomous and meaningful ways.

Victor Rios (2011) vividly describes how young minority men are labeled and criminalized. He argues that juvenile justice is part of a "youth control complex . . . where punishment threaded itself into the fabric of everyday social life in an array of institutions" (158). Likewise, Alice Goffman (2014) writes that the "young men around 6th Street [in Philadelphia] learn to fear far more than just the legal authorities. The reach of the police extends outward like a net around them—to public places in the city, to the activities they usually involve themselves in, and to the neighborhood spots where they can usually be found" (33–34). Jaime Fader (2013) observes that the juvenile justice system propagates a negative self-image. She maintains that "the facility . . . tells them, you are a criminal—that is, you are bad; you are the same as every other criminal found inside the facility's walls; . . . and you will likely always be that way" (14).

I perceived a different social dynamic. Juvenile justice in Boston and Chicago did not tirelessly track and observe teenagers. Especially an overwhelmed system like Chicago's could not effectively control the teenagers on probation. Even in Boston, Tyrell avoided getting caught for months before he was sent to a treatment center a second time. His mother was worried about him being on the streets, and we both speculated that the authorities might not be looking for him; Dorchester is comparatively small, so it was astonishing that the police didn't pick him up earlier. Nor did juvenile justice workers reinforce a negative self-image. Rather, they encouraged the teenagers to be overly optimistic. My results, however, also align with those of Rios, Fader, and A. Goffman in important ways. The teenagers in my study often failed to desist from crime, and they continued to struggle to become self-sufficient adults.

Poor communities in the United States have been segregated and neglected for decades (Massey and Denton 1993; Wilson 1990). Mass incarceration is just the latest aspect of a perpetual state of deprivation that encompasses those at the bottom of the socioeconomic ladder. The juvenile justice system is, in fact, the only social welfare institution that offered at least a modicum of support to the teenagers and the families I studied. At the same time, probation officers and caseworkers did not have the means to effectively address the teenagers' difficult social circumstances. The "American Dream" was therefore not a one-sided hegemonic discourse (Lincoln 1989). Teenagers and juvenile justice workers both relied on this narrative to avoid confronting the meaningless and artificial performances of incarceration, probation, and parole.

Amidst these macrosociological assessments my research also offers several concrete starting points for reconceptualizing juvenile justice policies. The teenagers unequivocally expressed a desire to act creatively in prosocial ways. Craving creative action is in line with the assessment that desistance can be achieved only if teenagers are able to make choices about their nondeviant self (Giordano, Cernkovich, and Rudolph 2002; Sampson and Laub 2005). Regrettably, juvenile justice in both cities offered only very limited opportunities for teenagers to experience creativity and agency within socially acceptable boundaries. In Chicago, scarce resources prevented the development of individual reentry plans. Teenagers were enrolled in programs based on availability rather than on their need. The Boston youth, in contrast, were overscheduled. While some welcomed the multiple programs they had to enroll in, others grew frustrated with their hectic life on the outside.

Comparing the two systems reveals that juvenile justice interventions ideally find the middle ground between allowing choice and exercising behavioral control. The data I collected show that interpersonal relationships between teenagers and juvenile justice workers are key for maintaining this delicate balance. Trust between a clinician and a client may help the latter to open up about temptations and struggles he faces without fearing reincarceration. Allowing teenagers to connect with one individual who stays with them throughout their time in the juvenile justice system (from pretrial detention to adjudication and reentry) also enables service providers to tailor programs to the teenagers' particular needs. Finally, juvenile justice programs should disconnect the teenagers' eligibility for social services from their risk assessment scores. Excluding teenagers who are, at least officially, not involved in serious crime defeats the system's capacity for early intervention.

Despite these tangible suggestions, I struggle with the practical relevance of my work. American sociologists have been studying urban poverty since the inception of the Chicago School in the early twentieth century (Burgess 1984; Park 1984). Over the past three decades many powerful urban ethnographies have uncovered the social dynamics at play in high-crime and high-poverty areas (A. Goffman 2014; Wacquant 2006; Bourgois 2002; Venkatesh 2002). Even though sociological research has demonstrated time and again the devastating impact of inequality and poverty, the social situation of the urban poor has not fundamentally changed. Weber (2002 [1904–5]) argued that the Puritans understood their economic success as a confirmation of their virtuous life choices (118). More than one hundred years after the first publication of *The Protestant Ethic*, US society still perceives poverty and its correlates crime and incarceration as an outcome of individual failure.

Recent political debates have developed around overt racism, particularly the excessive use of police force. This criticism is necessary, but it overlooks more subtle forms of marginalization that operate through narrative and governmental resource allocation. Acknowledging the need of inner-city minority teenagers to act creatively forces us to scrutinize the American mores of individualism, capitalism, and relentless success. If we want to improve the situation of young minority men, we need to accept their right to live fulfilled and meaningful lives just as middle-class children do.

Methodological
Reflections

During the first three years of my graduate studies I prepared myself to write a dissertation about Jewish resistance in German-occupied Europe during World War II. I had spent several years in Israel. I knew Hebrew and had already conducted preliminary research at the United States Holocaust Museum in Washington, DC. After I finished this first round of interviews and archival research, I realized that I did not want to study the Holocaust anymore. The Shoah and my own fragmented identity in relation to it had occupied my intellectual and professional development since my early teens. When I interviewed Holocaust survivors for my research, I needed to establish myself as a representative of a new, reformed Germany. I seemed to build trust easily with interviewees despite their initial skepticism. I was far too young to be implicated in the war crimes of Nazi Germany. I had lived in Israel and knew a lot about the Jewish culture the Nazis had destroyed. Talking to Holocaust survivors was nevertheless personal and painful. My grandparents were alive during the Third Reich, and like many Germans, I struggle to reconcile the love and respect I had for them with their— albeit passive—complicity in the extinction of European Jewry. I wanted to work on a topic unconnected to my own biography.

I started my research on Jewish resistance with the goal of understanding how people adapt to oppression, and after putting aside that research project, I was still interested in the same question. It is far too simplistic to equate the situation of European Jewry during World War II with marginalized urban populations in the United States. However, as I began to read more broadly about urban poverty, I noticed similarities between Jewish ghetto life during World War II and creative coping mechanisms of the urban poor (Bauer 2002; Stack 1973; Edin and Lein 1997). I believed that studying juvenile delinquency would allow me to pursue similar theoretical questions while also engaging with a contemporary and pressing social problem.

As I had hoped, the fact that I was German was not a liability anymore. I approached my fieldwork as an outsider who had not been socialized in the complex web of US race relations. The teenagers I recruited for my work were curious about my background and eager to ask questions about Germany. I did not have to manage my "Germanness" anymore; instead I had to come to terms with my role as woman in a male-dominated research setting.

GENDER AND FIELDWORK

At the beginning of the project, in the fall of 2009, I tried to establish a field site around a Catholic youth center in Englewood, looking for a way to access the network of young men who frequented the center. In a Chicago School manner, I wanted to become an apprentice. I was looking for a version of Elijah Anderson's "Herman" or Mitchell Duneier's "Hakim" who would serve as an inside track to the group of young men I was observing (Anderson 2003, 12; Duneier 2000, 11). I tried to become friends with one of the older teenagers—I will call him Jermaine—who had been a regular at the center for several years. He wanted to enroll in community college, so I began helping him with his applications. We started spending more time together at the field site. After a while he introduced me to his cousin, brother, and other friends. I was quite certain that I was on my way to building rapport and to being at least partially accepted in his circle of friends. Eventually, I asked him what he did on the weekends and if I could come with him and hang out. He replied, "That won't work. They [his friends] would just try to get with you."

His reaction made me uncomfortable. After all, I was married and was barely younger than his mother. Despite his blunt reply, I was not ready yet to give up on my plan of entering the world of this group of young men. I continued to spend time with Jermaine. I mostly helped him with homework assignments, hoping that eventually our relationship would reach a level of trust at which he would let me see the part of his life that I found most interesting: hanging out with his friends on the corner and hustling. But I never succeeded in receiving more than superficial introductions to his friends before we went our separate ways. One afternoon during our study session he told me frankly, "I want to have sex with you." Trying to emphasize my role as a wife and much older woman, I replied, "I have a husband and I could be your mother." That did not deter him from insisting that he just wanted to sleep with me once and that my husband would never have to know about it.

Jermaine had obviously misinterpreted my efforts to get to know him better, despite the fact that I had told him about my research project. The personal questions I had asked about his past involvement in crime, his family background, and his hopes for the future were seen within the framework of courtship. He perceived me as a peer who could potentially be a girlfriend or at least a one-night stand. I wanted to avoid such perceptions of my role. However, if I wanted the young men to trust me and open up about their internal lives, professional detachment did not seem a promising strategy. At the same time, it was quite obvious that I did not effectively negotiate the gendered scripts of interaction.

Another episode further illustrates how what I perceived to be allusions to my sexuality affected my interactions in the field. One young man I had talked to several times asked me if I could write him a letter that would confirm to his probation officer that he had done community service with me. I told him that I would not feel right doing so, because, in my view, hanging out with a graduate student from the University of Chicago does not qualify as giving back to the community that had been harmed by the crime he had committed. He started moving closer and his eyes wandered up and down, staring at me. He said, "Where did you get this black dress? You look real nice in it." Then he paused and added, "Come on, you can write that letter for me." It was a hot summer day. Almost no one was on the street, and we were sitting alone on the stoop in front of his grandmother's empty apartment. His brother had joined us and I felt outnumbered and cornered. Very likely nothing would have happened if I had not written the letter, but I was vulnerable enough to sit down and handwrite a note to get out of the situation as quickly as possible.

After several other more or less explicit sexual advances from youths I interacted with, I realized that I needed to manage my gender just as I had earlier managed my German heritage. I developed more structured ways of engaging with the young men that would place me in a more professional context. I abandoned my attempts to observe them in an open-ended way at the Catholic youth center. Beginning in March 2010 I became an intern at the Scholarship and Guidance Association. SGA supported my data collection, and I was able to recruit additional teenagers for my dissertation work. The interviews initially took place at the young men's school.

Unlike my previous data-gathering attempts, in this setting, I had a clearly defined role. The boundaries between me and the young men were almost impermeable, which protected me but also significantly limited the data I could collect. I continued my interviews at the school until the summer break of 2010, during which I began to interview the young men in their homes. The coordination of these visits often took place through their female guardians because most teenagers I interviewed did not own a cell phone.

When I was at the young men's homes, usually I did not interact very much with their mothers, grandmothers, sisters, or aunts before or after the interview. When I entered their houses or apartments, the women often referred to me as a social worker. I was allowed into their homes, but my access was restricted to a specific engagement with the young men. For instance, one of the mothers, who would later generously hand down baby clothes and invite me to her daughter's first birthday party, initially barely acknowledged my presence. When I entered the house, she usually sat on the sofa, holding her newborn. After a brief "How are you doing?" she yelled to her son, "Michaela is here!" While I waited for her son to appear, I tried several times to begin a conversation about her new daughter. I mentioned how cute her baby was, but no further conversation developed. She told me to take a seat in the dining area and went back to watching TV. I felt like an outsider treated with reserved friendliness. Consequently, my data collection was limited to what the young men talked about in the interviews.

I was self-conscious about my lack of immersion in the community. During the defense of my dissertation proposal a member of my committee brought up Alice Goffman's piece recently published in the *American Sociological Review* and her ability to deeply immerse herself in the world of young inner-city men. I felt attacked and became defensive. I had tried to do what she did but had failed.

In retrospect, my committee members were encouraging, but I couldn't shake off a sense of failure. A few days later, one of my advisors, Bernard Harcourt, called me into his office to talk about the implications of our meeting. He reiterated that I did not have to hang out in crack houses or dark alleyways to write a good dissertation; and he made clear that the path I had chosen was perfectly reasonable for the research questions I wanted to answer. Bernard's encouragement meant a lot to me on a personal level, but it was even more important professionally. He gave me the permission to be self-confident about my methods even if I was not deeply embedded in the community I studied.

Much of the well-known qualitative work on crime and poverty in the United States is based on ethnographies in which the researcher took on the role of an apprentice (Venkatesh 2008; Wacquant 2006; Duneier 2000; Anderson 2003; Bourgois 2002). Loïc Wacquant, for example, argues for a "carnal" sociology. He suggests that embedding oneself completely is the ultimate form of data collection. It "allows us to probe into the makeup of habitus by studying not its products but its production." Wacquant elaborates that immersion also captures the "visceral" quality of social life that "standard modes of social inquiry typically purge from their accounts" (Wacquant 2005, 465).

"Going native" in spectacular ways often generates a narrative more easily accessible for lay readers. Urban ethnographies tend to reach a readership beyond the narrow world of academia. Sudhir Venkatesh's *Gang Leader for a Day* (2008), for example, was featured prominently in the popular press. More recently, Alice Goffman's *On the Run* (2014) became a national best seller, and her Ted Talk on mass incarceration has been viewed almost a million times. During cocktail hours of annual conferences, or lately in anonymous online forums, sociologists may express skepticism about the ethics of Venkatesh's and Goffman's work. At the same time, many consider complete immersion via the apprentice role the gold standard for qualitative work. "Talk," as Colin Jerolmack and Shamus Khan (2014) argue, is "cheap." Interviews, they suggest, can't validly account for people's actions the way observations do. They rightly point out that some research questions cannot be answered via interview data. Yet their controversial article also implies that ethnography may be the only way sociologists can uncover the contingencies of social action.

Female sociologists who want to observe culture in action in a male-dominated setting have to walk a fine line. Flirting with an informant can open avenues of inquiry. Yet using female charisma to gain access to a field site is not only physically risky; it also builds very fragile social relationships. Aside from ethical considerations, losing access to a field site is a distinct possibility if a woman does not deliver on her unspoken promise of mutual attraction. Negotiating the demands that men make on their bodies is par for the course for female ethnographers (Mazzei and O'Brien 2009). Realizing that I did not have the fortitude to embed myself deeply in the lifeworlds of delinquent teenagers brought a feeling of personal failure. Yet, as my work developed, I learned that "carnal connections" and "going native" are not the only ways to collect nuanced and in-depth data about the life of juvenile offenders.

While I collected data in Chicago, I underwent the ultimate female bodily and role transformation. I became pregnant and gave birth to my oldest daughter. In many cases the researcher can only speculate about how his or her social and demographic attributes influence data collection. My pregnancy provided me with the unique opportunity to take on a new social role and to compare the process of data gathering to my previous attempts. My Chicago field site did not change, and the young men I interacted with remained the same. However, as I became a mother, I stopped trying to access the masculine space that I thought was the cradle of juvenile delinquency. Instead my mother role allowed me to connect with the female lifeworld that surrounded the young men I studied.

BECOMING A MOTHER

Other female scholars have previously observed the transforming role that motherhood has in disadvantaged communities. In *Honor and the American Dream* (1992), Ruth Horowitz argues that motherhood can resolve the conflict young women in disadvantaged inner-city neighborhoods feel between being abstinence and being labeled a "loose woman." Becoming a mother meant that young women's actions were interpreted within a new framework, and in the eyes of their community, their actions had different meaning (130). Similarly, Carol Stack (1974) describes how being pregnant eased her own entrance into the field in her study of kinship ties in a disadvantaged inner-city community (8). She confirms that her research subjects considered becoming a mother to be honorable and deserving of respect, even at a young age (46–47).[1]

In my case, becoming a mother changed not only how I was perceived but also how I interacted with the young men and their families. Evoking the mother role to generate commonality was now plausible, and referring to frames of motherhood allowed me to transcend class boundaries. As a result, I interacted more confidently with other mothers and their children. The confidence and plausibility of my role was reciprocated by increasing trust and willingness on the part of the mothers and their sons to share their daily struggles with me.

Simultaneously, my transformation affected the frames I used to make sense of the environment I observed (E. Goffman 1986). Three specific changes are visible in my field notes. First, becoming a mother allowed me to desexualize my interactions with the young men, enabling me to build rapport without being considered a potential love interest. Second, evoking the mother role in a plausible way allowed me to build relationships with female household members who previously had no interest in extended interaction with me. Third, observing how the young men interacted with my daughter and other younger siblings allowed me to see an unexpected caring side to the young men.

The struggles I had experienced early on in maintaining boundaries while still collecting in-depth data disappeared when I became a mother. The transcripts of my interviews show that the conversations I had with the young men became more penetrating. In March 2011, for example, Ben, who was seventeen years old, was talking about his pregnant girlfriend. He had just felt the baby move for the first time. I shared how I felt when I saw my daughter's face on an ultrasound image for the first time. When I then asked him about his goals as a father, he replied, "To be a good father and to take care and to do everything I didn't get." I asked him what makes someone a good father.

BEN: Being there for him [his son]. Being able to take care of his [a father's] responsibilities, that is how it is supposed to be.

M.S.:   And you think your dad never did that for you?

BEN: Not all his responsibilities. I don't know. There is a lot of stuff he ain't do.

M.S.:   So what would you wish your dad would have done for you?

BEN: Stayed in my life.

This was the first time Ben ever talked about his father abandoning him when he was a little boy. When he talked about his father before, he usually mentioned only how much he liked spending time with him and his half-siblings. Ben and I had an intimate conversation about being parents. At the same time, our exchange was desexualized. Within this framework of mutual trust, I was able to learn about an important biographical detail that he had not shared before.

Not only did my relationship with the teenagers change significantly, but I was also able to build rapport with the mothers whom I encountered before or after interviews. Michael was the youngest boy in my sample. He had just turned fifteen. His mother was my age, in her early thirties. She had two older children, a girl and another boy, both in their late teens. Michael lived with his mother, two siblings, and various other family members in his grandmother's apartment on the far South Side of Chicago. When Michael violated the terms of his probation because he missed his curfew, he was sent to a drug rehabilitation facility an hour and half away from Chicago. Since Michael's mother did not have a car and the place was almost impossible to reach by public transportation, I offered to drive her. On our way back from the facility we began talking about motherhood.

> M.S.: Becoming a mother is crazy. I have never loved anyone as much as I love Rebekka [my daughter]. I would throw myself under the bus for her. I have never felt that way before about anyone, not even my husband.

> MICHAEL'S MOTHER: I would do anything for my children. Anything. I can't understand how women can say, "I hate my child because I hate his father." I hate Michael's father. He a deadbeat. But I always say, "The best thing I got out of that relationship is Michael."

I brought up having overheard some mothers at juvenile court making negative statements about their children and finding it very disturbing to witness mothers say such things.

> MICHAEL'S MOTHER: Yeah, some women say, "Take him; I don't want him. He should go to DOC [Department of Corrections]." I am like, "You want your kid in prison? That is not a place to be for him." Some mothers don't even show up for court anymore. I can't understand. I always went for Michael, and I don't want him to be locked up.

In this case, motherhood gave me a framework within which to interact with another woman who was sociodemographically very different from me. Our lifeworlds intersected when we affirmed the love we felt for our children. Starting the conversation by affirming my own motherhood and the feelings related to it encouraged Michael's mother to disclose her feelings as well. Michael's mother then opened up about her personal life, her difficulties finding her own apartment, and her complicated relationship with her current partner.

I realized that she did not have a lot of emotional resources for parenting her youngest child. She was also unhappy with the cramped conditions the family lived in, yet was unable to provide her son with sufficient space.[2] In terms of understanding Michael's trajectory of desistance and recidivism, it became clear to me that Michael did not have an emotionally supportive mother. Although she loved her son, she was preoccupied with getting the very basic aspects of her life in order, such as stabilizing her relationship with her husband and finding a new apartment. Michael was on his own when it came to facing the challenges of growing up in a high-crime neighborhood.

In addition to helping build rapport with mothers, motherhood also changed the interpretative frames I used to understand the social environment I observed. Darrius, on probation for armed robbery, was one of the chronically unreliable youths in my sample. I usually had to wait about twenty minutes at his home before either he appeared or I left because none of his family could track him down. Darrius's family lived in one of the mixed-income units that had replaced the infamous Cabrini Green projects. During one visit, his cousin and her two children, a nine-month-old and a three-year-old, were sitting in the kitchen together with Darrius's sister. They stayed in one of the bedrooms in the house. Darrius's younger brother and sister were sitting in front of the TV. Darrius's cousin prepared food for her infant daughter by pouring pink juice mix into a bottle.

While I was waiting for Darrius to show up, I told the cousin that I had a two-month-old daughter myself and that I was breast-feeding her. She replied, "Yeah, I was not gonna do that. No way. They tried to convince me at the hospital to breast-feed! They crazy! Feed every two hours. No way. I started mixing cereal into her formula when she was eight weeks old. They sleep better, you know." We continued talking about the pros and cons of breast-feeding while Darrius's sister made calls to find out where her brother was. In the meantime, the older child had begun nagging his mother, trying to get her attention. He started whining, "Mom, Mom, Mom!" and tugged on her pants. She ignored him at first, but when his whining became louder, she raised her voice and reprimanded him: "I told you to leave me alone!" He immediately backed off and quietly sat down in front of the TV. We continued our conversation about food, and Darrius's cousin emphasized that her daughter could hold her own bottle but that she was just sometimes too lazy to do it herself. Darrius never showed up that day. I left after half an hour.

On my way home I dwelled on the fact that Darrius's cousin would not follow the doctor's advice about breast-feeding, holding back cereal, and avoiding juice. I was also surprised by the authoritarian way she interacted with her older son, who was clamoring for her attention. To make sense of her choices, I compared my privileged position as a middle-class mother to an only child with the living situation of Darrius's family.

Nine people were living in that five-bedroom apartment. Darrius had an older sister, two little sisters, and a little brother. His cousin had two children, and his mother lived there as well. For his cousin, keeping everyone disciplined and minimizing work were paramount concerns. One could argue that she was simply not aware of the benefits of breast-feeding, but her living situation and the presence of a lot of children must have made it very difficult to sustain the practice. Having a child sleep through the night also becomes more important when people live in close quarters.

Because I was attuned to the feeding of babies, I was aware of the choices she had made and the implications those choices had for the household and her child. I had experienced firsthand how much work it is to mother an infant, and by comparing my choices to those of Darrius's cousin, I was able to understand that the time spent on each child in his household had to be limited.

I realized that parenting in Darrius's home was similar to the style that Annette Lareau describes in *Unequal Childhoods* (2011). According to Lareau, poor families tend to use directives rather than discussing disciplinary decisions with their children. Their parenting decisions are confined by time constraints and the desire to keep things simple (146–47). The fact that Darrius's cousin told her son to be quiet instead of engaging with him, and her desire for the baby to sleep through the night early in her development, clearly reflects such constraints. If we assume that Darrius's mother used the same parenting strategies as the cousin used with her children, what this dynamic meant for Darrius's development as a teenager is that he did not receive a lot of guidance or supervision from his family. Parenting was reserved for the younger children. I began to understand why it was so difficult for Darrius to stick to his plan to stay in the house and focus on school. He could leave any time, and nobody seemed to mind that he did not keep his curfew. The adults in the home were busy taking care of the younger children.

The largest impact motherhood had on my fieldwork affected the ways I observed the young men themselves. In some instances, I had to bring my daughter with me when I conducted interviews. Her presence changed the interview dynamic as she became the focus of attention. Not only did the female household members hover over her, but the young men also showed interest in interacting with her. For one of my last meetings with Dan, I brought my six-month-old daughter with me and put her on the living room floor. She had just started sitting up but was still unstable. Dan looked at me in astonishment. "You can't let your baby sit on the floor without putting pillows around. She is gonna fall." He then got several pillows, put them down around her. He squatted on the floor, holding her and making sure that she didn't fall over. An experienced babysitter, Dan had a year-old sister whom he babysat regularly, and he also looked after his three-year-old nephew.

I witnessed a similar moment with Trevor. His mother had invited me and my daughter to his little sister's birthday party. Trevor, who struggled with his anger and violent outbursts, carried his little sister around, playing with her. And, most astonishingly for a sixteen-year-old boy, he spent a whole Saturday with his family at his sister's first birthday party. I joked that I could use a babysitter and that Trevor seemed to be really into his sister. His mother, who usually did not hold back on the problems she experienced with her son, explained to me, "You can trust him with children. Trevor is good with kids. Kids like him. He knows how to take care of them. He always plays nicely with his little sister. He loves her."

Becoming a mother fundamentally changed my subjective involvement in the social world that I was trying to observe and interpret. Having a child allowed me to plausibly evoke the mother role, which inevitably altered how I interacted with the teenagers and their families. Consequently it also changed how I was perceived by them (E. Goffman 1986, 13; Horowitz 1992, 130–31). None of the teenagers ever tried to approach me sexually again. I was perceived within the "mother" framework rather than in the "girlfriend" category. I also collected data markedly different from what I had set out to gather. Instead of observing "corner boy" behavior (A. Cohen 1955), I saw the home lives of the teenagers. I saw how the "macho" side that I observed in group settings melted away when they were at home engaging with my daughter or their little siblings and cousins.

INSTITUTIONAL BARRIERS

While I conducted my fieldwork in Chicago, my husband finished his PhD and took a faculty position at Wellesley College. In the attempt to make virtue out of necessity, I decided set up a second field site. After I had spent two years researching juvenile justice in Chicago, I moved to Boston in the fall of 2011.

Recruiting teenagers was easier than it had been in Chicago. Through personal contacts to a juvenile judge in the Metro West area, I arranged a meeting with Jane Tewksbury, the DYS commissioner at the time. She was in general positively disposed toward research at the DYS, and my fieldwork was approved quickly. With DYS support I recruited eight teenagers at the Eliot Detention Center in Dorchester.

In Chicago it had been impossible for me to get the JTDC's cooperation. Despite declining incarceration rates, the JTDC remained an eyesore for the city, causing negative publicity. As the institution had been more or less under siege for several decades, it was not a surprise that midlevel administrators were not particularly eager to support my desire to engage in a long-term observational and interview study there. Instead of working with the JTDC, I recruited teenagers through the social work provider I interned with, as well as through the Catholic youth center that I at first believed would be the focal point of my work.

After the initial hurdles, data collection in Chicago progressed smoothly. I realized that the most effective way of reconnecting with teenagers who had ceased to be SGA clients was to meet them at juvenile court during one of their dispositions. While I waited with the youths outside the courtroom for their case to be called, I often encountered their probation officers. I introduced myself as a PhD student from the University of Chicago. All of the probation officers I met were open-minded about my desire to do in-depth research with their clients. Two POs even encouraged me to call them about updates concerning their clients. They explained to me that they see any kind of attention the teenagers get from a well-meaning adult as positive. Teenagers also asked me to come into the courtroom with them, and judges usually did not object once I offered my business card and disclosed my intention to study recidivism and desistance.

The probation officers' openness to my research was indicative of their overwhelming caseloads. POs gave me special permission to visit the teenagers at group homes and at times connected me with parents or legal guardians. My continuous presence allowed me to become a resource for them. In one case, for example, a probation officer asked me to get in touch with a child to inform him about the state of his case and to remind him to check in.

Inadvertently, I had thus taken a bottom-up approach in Chicago to access the different juvenile justice institutions. By building rapport with probation officers, I was able to follow the teenagers through the system and keep track of their different placements and probation requirements. Although the Chicago system seemed closed to me at the higher administrative levels, those who worked with teenagers on a day-to-day basis often felt the shortcomings of the system acutely. They perceived me as "being on their side." My interactions with parents developed in very similar ways. None of the parents I approached refused to give consent for their sons' participation. On the contrary, they were pleased by the fact that another adult had taken an interest in their children and hoped that participation in my research study would encourage their sons to stay out of trouble.

Needless to say, after I had cleared the institutional barriers so quickly in Chicago, I expected no further complications when I began work in Boston. Building on my experience in Chicago, I made an effort to connect with caseworkers, who had the role of probation officers for adjudicated teenagers in Boston. I quickly learned that my research was perceived as an intrusion. Unlike probation officers in Chicago, caseworkers in Boston were concerned about defending their professional turf and seemed threatened by an outsider who wanted to engage with their clients. In fact, adopting the language of "caring for the teenagers" was seen as an infringement on the caseworker's expertise. One of the caseworkers, for example, insistently tried to minimize my interaction with one of her clients, who had enrolled in the study. In a phone conversation she told me that I had no right to speak with her client and that it was for her to decide whether I would be able to continue my research with him. As a result of the caseworkers' intervention, the DYS's Internal Review Board significantly reduced my access to the teenagers. I was originally allowed to meet with them weekly, but at the beginning of March 2012 my interviews were cut back to once a month, and I was not able to gather observational data outside the immediate interview situation. Teenagers not in DYS custody were not affected by this regulation, and I could continue to meet them as regularly as I had before.

Receiving parental consent was also more challenging in Boston than in Chicago. While the teenagers in Chicago were clearly underserved, the Boston youths had to deal with an array of social workers, street workers, probation officers, and caseworkers. Parents seemed more skeptical of additional outside attention. Four mothers I approached did not consent to their teenagers' participation. Two of those were positively disposed to the project initially, but later let me know that they had received advice from their sons' lawyer or social worker not to let their sons participate in a research study. Thus, regrettably, the data in Boston are not as in-depth as those for Chicago. I could recruit only eight teenagers, about half the number I had hoped to achieve. On the other hand, I was able to interview young men while they were being held in detention or prison facilities, which was impossible in Chicago because of the lack of institutional support.

The differences I experienced as I was trying to set up my field sites revealed major disparities between the two systems. The Chicago juvenile justice system lacked the resources to provide comprehensive social services and did not supervise the teenagers after their release as intensively as the DYS in Boston. Chicago's practitioners were aware of the systems' shortcomings and were grateful for what they perceived as additional support. Administrators, on the other hand, had no interest in inviting further scrutiny of their already embattled system. The Boston system had more financial resources. It was a highly professionalized institution in which "caring for" juvenile offenders required specialized skills and qualifications. "Caretaking" specialists managed different parts of the teenagers' lives. While administrators were glad to let researchers observe what they perceived as a relatively progressive, rehabilitation-centered juvenile justice system, some social workers and caseworkers were suspicious of an outsider who could potentially challenge their professional authority.

Both systems showed less interest in those teenagers who had not been arrested for severe crimes. In Chicago, parents and probation officers were even more eager to have me involved in such cases, since the lack of criminality meant that teenagers had hardly any social service resources at their disposal. In Boston, teenagers deemed "less dangerous" were usually not committed to the DYS but remained, supervised by a probation officer, under the jurisdiction of the juvenile court and probation department. They did not receive comprehensive attention from a caseworker and often bounced back and forth between home and the Eliot Detention Center. This lack of streamlined rehabilitative services again translated into parents being more forthcoming and open about their sons' participation in my research. I had more leeway during the data collection process because I did not infringe on the authority of a caseworker or other social worker who had been assigned to the teenager.

As the tables below show, the distribution of interviews in Boston is very different from Chicago. Participants are fewer, but since I was able to regularly interview the teenagers while they were in the DYS custody, the interviews per person are more numerous and more evenly distributed. At the same time, the data in Boston suffer from my inability to gather observational data in multiple settings. My depiction of the Boston cases thus relies much more on the interview data and less on participant observation than the narrative I am able to provide about the Chicago group. Demographically, it is interesting to note that the Boston cases are more racially diverse than in Chicago, which is a testimony to the overall greater ethnic diversity in Boston. Furthermore, I happened to recruit more teenagers who come from intact families in Boston than in Chicago. Yet, due to the small number of participants, I cannot confidently draw any broader conclusions about this difference.

CONCLUSION: IMPERFECTIONS AND REGRETS

"If you could go back in time, what would you do differently?" was usually one of the initial questions I asked when I interviewed a teenagers for the first time. Now, six years into this project, I inevitably have to ask myself the same question. If I could go back and change anything, I would not waste my time emulating other ethnographies of street life. I would focus even more on the nondeviant aspects of the teenagers' lives. I regret that I did not engage systematically with the adults, juvenile justice officials, relatives, and caretakers who surrounded the young men. More often than I would like to admit, I pursued any data that I could get, rather than thinking systematically about the data that I still needed in relation to the material I had already gathered. After negotiating gender roles and institutional obstacles, turning data into prose feels like the final act of impression management. I am tempted to present my research process as a well-defined path to completion, rather than a rocky and unpredictable road that took sudden turns and more than once seemed to end nowhere.

Crispin Birnbaum, then the general counsel of the DYS in Boston, asked me during a meeting, how I knew that the teenagers were telling me the truth. At the time, I was irritated because she seemed to imply that as a lawyer she was more effective in retrieving the "truth" than I was as a sociologist. Now, with the necessary distance from the anxieties and excitement of the field, I understand that striving for some version of the "truth" is meaningless. Instead I was able to collect several idiosyncratic versions of reality. My own perceptions of the field were contingent on my life circumstances and the role transformations I underwent. Likewise, the young men I interviewed reassessed their motives and adapted their actions to the fluid conditions of their social environment. As I analyzed the data, I tried to extract the ways in which these different realities intersect and

Table 1   List of Participants, Chicago

	Age at enrollment	Criminal history*	Crime committed at enrollment in study*	Type of incarceration	Racial/ethnic background	Number of interviews	Enrollment in study
Ben	17	Status offenses, trespassing	Unlawful use of a weapon	Secure detention, group home, Cook County Jail	African American	13	July 2010– May 2013
Dan	15	Drug dealing	Unlawful use of a weapon, domestic violence	Secure detention, group home	African American	18	July 2010– May 2012
Demetrius	15	Robbery, assault and battery	Robbery, assault and battery	Secure detention, group home, Cook County Jail	African American	10	July 2010– May 2012
Miguel	16	Gang affiliated	Domestic violence	Psychiatric hospital, secure detention, group home	Latino	4	April 2011– May 2012
Trevor	16	Robbery, assault and battery	Robbery, assault and battery	Secure detention, group home	African American	25	July 2010– May 2012
Damon	17	Armed robbery	Armed robbery	Secure detention, group home, Cook County Jail, prison	African American	8	July 2010– May 2012
Darrius	15	Theft, armed robbery	Armed robbery	Secure detention, group home, juvenile prison	African American	13	August 2010– May 2012
Delane	17	Armed robbery	Armed robbery	Secure detention, Cook County Jail, prison	African American	5	July 2010– August 2010
Jamal	15	Theft, status offenses (smoking marijuana, not attending school)	Theft	Secure detention, group home, Cook County Jail, prison	African American	15	July 2010– May 2012

Name	Age	Self-reported	Official charge	Institution	Race/Ethnicity	Number	Interview dates
James	16	Gang affiliated	Unlawful use of a weapon	Secure detention, group home	African American	13	August 2010–December 2011
Kendrick	17	Unarmed robbery, drug dealing	Unarmed robbery	Secure detention, group home	African American	8	July 2010–April 2011
Marvin	17	Armed robbery	Armed robbery	Secure detention, group home, Cook County Jail, prison	African American	6	August 2010–October 2010
Michael	14	Theft, assault and battery, status offenses (smoking marijuana, not attending school)	Theft	Secure detention, group home, drug rehabilitation	African American	7	March 2011–June 2011
Peter	17	None	Drug dealing	Cook County Jail	African American	5	March 2011–May 2011
Robert	15	Status offenses loosely gang affiliated	Smoking marijuana	Group home	Latino	9	March 2011–May 2012

*As reported by the participant.

Table 2 List of Participants, Boston

	Age at enrollment	Criminal history*	Crime committed at enrollment in study*	Type of incarceration	Racial/ethnic background	Number of interviews	Enrollment in study
Darell	15	Theft, status offenses (smoking marijuana, not keeping curfew at home)	Theft, assault and battery	Secure detention, group home	African American	18	February 2012– March 2013
Demarco	17	Armed robbery	Armed robbery	Secure detention, treatment center	Caribbean	10	October 2011– February 2013
Jason	17	Gang involvement	Unlawful use of a weapon	Secure detention, juvenile treatment center	African American	19	September 2011– June 2013
Javon	17	Gang involvement	Unlawful use of a weapon	Secure detention, juvenile treatment center	African American	18	September 2011– March 2013
Jose	15	Dealing drugs, theft	Unarmed robbery	Secure detention	Latino	14	April 2012– December 2012
Lamar	16	Unarmed robbery	Unlawful use of a weapon	Secure detention, juvenile treatment center	African American	7	October 2011– February 2013
Lucas	16	Theft, armed robbery	Accessory to armed robbery	Secure detention	Latino	30	February 2012– June 2012
Tyrell	15	Dealing drugs, theft	Theft	Secure detention, juvenile treatment center	African American/ Latino	17	September 2012– March 2013

*As reported by the participant.

corroborate each other. The conclusions I have drawn are therefore far from being a definite verdict on the state of the juvenile justice system. I hope, however, that my work offers a new perspective on a pressing topic, and that this book inspires others to collect new data, which may be used to challenge, refine, and develop the material I have presented.

Notes

INTRODUCTION

1. The number of respondents who continue to believe in the "American Dream" has declined to 64 percent from 72 percent in 2009. Yet this downward trend remains within the boundaries of up- and downward movements over the past few decades. Sorkin and Thee-Brenan.

2. The presence of a dominating discourse does not preclude the existence of counter-hegemonic narratives. As Bruce Lincoln and others have pointed out, the oppressed make quite effective use of myth and narrative to further their independence and remain creative agents (Bauer 2002; Scott 1992; Lincoln 1989; Scott 1986). The young men I studied were also exposed to discourses that countered the dominating narrative of the *American Dream*. Deviance itself could, for example, be framed as resistance against oppression (Cohen 2004).

2. TWO CITIES, TWO SYSTEMS, SIMILAR PROBLEMS

1. "Sites and Contacts," Juvenile Detention Alternatives Initiative, Annie E. Casey Foundation, http://www.aecf.org/work/juvenile-justice/jdai/ (accessed February 20, 2016).

2. Juvenile Detention Alternatives Initiative, "Draft: 2011 Annual Results Report," Annie E. Casey Foundation, February 25, 2013, http://www.aecf.org/m/resourcedoc/aecf-JDAIResults2011-2013.pdf (accessed March 27, 2016).

3. Massachusetts joined the JDAI in 2006.

4. See "Easy Access to the Census of Juveniles in Residential Placement," US Office of Juvenile Justice and Delinquency Prevention, http://www.ojjdp.gov /ojstatbb/ezacjrp/ (accessed February 20, 2013).

5. "Public Information Packet," Department of Youth Services, Mass.gov (Massachusetts state government website), 2013, http://www.mass.gov/eohhs /docs/dys/public-info-packet.pdf (copy in author's possession).

6. "About Us," Illinois Department of Juvenile Justice, http://www.illinois .gov/idjj/Pages/AboutUs.aspx (accessed March 25, 2012).

7. "About the Court," State of Illinois, Circuit Court of Cook County, http:// www.cookcountycourt.org/ABOUTTHECOURT/JuvenileJusticeChildProtection /JuvenileJustice.aspx (accessed March 25, 2016).

8. "Juvenile Justice and Child Protection Department," State of Illinois, Circuit Court of Cook County, http://www.cookcountycourt.org/ABOUTTHECOURT /JuvenileJusticeChildProtection.aspx (accessed November 13, 2012).

9. According to Massachusetts general law, a "child in need of services" is "a child between the ages of 6 and 17 who: (a) repeatedly runs away from the home of a parent or legal guardian; (b) repeatedly fails to obey the lawful and reasonable commands of a parent or legal guardian, thereby interfering with the parent's or legal guardian's ability to adequately care for and protect the child; (c) repeatedly fails to obey lawful and reasonable school regulations; or (d) when not otherwise excused from attendance in accordance with lawful and reasonable school regulations, willfully fails to attend school for more than eight school days in a quarter." Mass. Gen. Laws Ann., ch. 119, sec. 21. In November 2012 CHINS was replaced with the Child Requiring Assistance Law (CRA). All teenagers in this study were still subject to the old CHINS law. CRA is less punitive than CHINS and is supposed to divert children from legal procedures (see Michael F. Kilkelly "Lawyers Journal: CHINS Reform; What the Statute Changes Mean for Your Practice," MassBar Association, February 2013, http://www.massbar.org /publications/lawyers-journal/2013/february/chins-reform-what-the-statute-changes-mean-for-your-practice (accessed August 4, 2015).

10. Two of the Chicago teenagers had to remain at the Saura Center for more than four months because DCFS was unable to find a permanent place for them to live. The maximum time teenagers are supposed to stay at the Saura Center was thirty days.

11. When I started my research at the Saura Center during the spring of 2010, there were only male residents. During the 2010–11 school year, girls were added to the population.

12. See Massachusetts Department of Youths Services, "2012 Grid: Most Frequently Cited Offenses," Committee for Public Counsel Services, June 26, 2012, https://www.publiccounsel.net/ya/wp-content/uploads/sites/6/2015/02/DYS2012 Grid.pdf (accessed March 25, 2016).

13. On February 22, 2013, Illinois closed its only maximum-security facility for juveniles in Joliet, Illinois. The prisoners were transferred to one of the seven remaining locations. The closure was motivated by budget cuts. See "Last Day at Last Prison in Joliet," *Herald-News (Joliet)*, February 22, 2013.

14. "IJJC Youth Reentry Improvement Report," Illinois Juvenile Justice Commission, Illinois Department of Human Services, http://www.dhs.state .il.us/page.aspx?item=58025 (accessed October 23, 2013).

3. TOO LITTLE TOO LATE

1. The Scholarship and Guidance Association (SGA) was a social work agency that did rehabilitative programming with young men on probation.

2. Jamal alleged that his uncle abused him and his siblings, but DCFS found the accusation to be unsubstantiated.

3. Darryl worked for a mentoring program at Jamal's school. His probation officer had arranged for Jamal's enrollment in the program.

4. His grandmother told me once that she suspected Jamal's problems were related to the fact that his mother had taken crack while she was pregnant with him.

4. IMAGINING DESISTANCE

1. While the law clearly distinguishes between theft and robbery, I use the term "robbery" or "rob" when the youths used it to refer to their actions, irrespective of their actual crime.

2. Job Corps is a technical training and education program designed for young people at least sixteen years of age who qualify as low income. The program is administered by the US Department of Labor. See http://www.jobcorps .gov/home.aspx for more information.

5. WEAK TIES—STRONG EMOTIONS

1. Reflecting the nationwide trend, minority youths were overrepresented in the Boston juvenile justice system. In 2011 64.3 percent of all youths held in juvenile facilities nationwide were black or Hispanic. See Sickmund, M., T.J. Sladky, W. Kang, and C. Puzzanchera (2013), "Easy Access to the Census of Juveniles in Residential Placement," Office of Juvenile Justice and Delinquency Prevention, http://www.ojjdp.gov/ojstatbb/ezacjrp/ (accessed February 27, 2016).

2. The young men may have avoided the issue of racial inequality because I am white. On the other hand, I had good rapport with most of the teenagers.

They felt comfortable talking about sensitive topics and had, for example, no qualms asking about my German heritage and Germany's Nazi past.

3. In 2007, the JTDC in Chicago changed the hiring requirements for staff who supervise teenagers on the unit. Youth development specialists, as the line staff are officially referred to, are now required to hold at minimum a bachelor's degree. At the time of my research Eric Dunlap, the interim administrator of the JTDC, was struggling with the union to implement the increase in educational requirements and to lay off staff who did not meet the new requirements. See Lisa Donovan, "Juvenile Detention Staffers Face Crackdown," *Chicago Sun-Times*, July 4, 2009, reposted at http://www.suffredin.org/news/newsitem.asp?language=english&newsitemid=3838 (accessed April 4, 2016).

4. It is important to note, though, that favoritism and arbitrariness were not limited to entry-level juvenile justice workers. In Boston, teenagers mentioned what they perceived as unfair treatment from the assistant director of the Eliot Detention Center. When Javon arrived at Eliot, he at first believed that the assistant director was "cool, but then six months in he was just a jerk. . . . He says that he is gonna do something, have a cookout or something, and then he forgets. And you are like, 'Hey, you just told us two days ago; how could you forget?'" Jason had the impression that the assistant director was "bipolar." According to Jason, he was usually very nice but could turn abruptly and act as if he didn't know you at all.

7. "I KNOW HOW TO CONTROL MYSELF"

1. Like the South Side of Chicago, Dorchester encompasses a large area with different levels of poverty. Comparing the area around Washington Park on Chicago's South Side to the gentrifying part of Dorchester around the Savin Hill subway stop may exaggerate the differences between the two places. Yet even the poorest areas in Dorchester that I visited, around Blue Course Drive and the Lincoln Park Zoo, were still in much better condition than the impoverished areas in Englewood section of Chicago's South Side, which I frequented during my fieldwork.

2. In 2009 Washington Park marked the boundary of the University of Chicago's gentrification efforts.

3. None of the Boston youths I interviewed appeared when I searched for their names in the publicly available inmate database of the Massachusetts Department of Corrections. It is safe to assume that as of November 2015 none of the teenagers I interviewed in Boston were serving time in a state penitentiary in Massachusetts. The Boston juvenile justice system has the option to commit youths to the juvenile system until they are twenty-one. DYS did not respond to my requests for an update about the youths whom I interviewed, so I am unable

to verify with official data whether or not the teenagers in Boston desisted from crime or recidivated and remain under DYS supervision. When I sought to reconnect with parents and guardians of the youths, I succeeded with three out of eight participants. I found that two of those three had recidivated and had spent time again at a juvenile justice facility after the study was finished.

4. I once joked with a DYS staff member who had worked with Jason that I did not understand how he had ended up in the DYS, because he was so laid-back and quiet. The staff member wholeheartedly agreed with me.

APPENDIX

1. For a more recent study about the role of motherhood in disadvantaged inner-city communities, see Edin and Kefalas (2005).

2. Michael had to share a bed with his uncle. His mother usually slept on blankets spread out on the floor of the living room.

References

Abrams, Laura. 2012. "Envisioning Life 'On the Outs': Exit Narratives of Incarcerated Male Youth." *International Journal of Offender Therapy and Comparative Criminology* 56 (6): 877–96.

Agnew, Robert. "Foundation for a General Strain Theory of Crime and Delinquency." *Criminology* 1 (1992): 47–88.

Anderson, Elijah. 2003. *A Place on the Corner.* 2nd ed. Chicago: University of Chicago Press.

Alexander, Michelle. 2012. *The New Jim Crow.* New York: New Press.

Bauer, Yehuda. 2002. *Rethinking the Holocaust.* New Haven, CT: Yale University Press.

Blau, Peter M. 1986. *Exchange and Power in Social Life.* Piscataway, NJ: Transaction.

Bourdieu, Pierre. 1984. *Distinction. A Social Critique of the Judgment of Taste.* Cambridge, MA: Harvard University Press.

Bourgois, Philippe. 2002. *In Search of Respect: Selling Crack in El Barrio.* 2nd ed. New York: Cambridge University Press.

Burgess, Ernest. 1984. "The Growth of the City: An Introduction to a Research Project." In *The City,* 47–62. By Robert Park, Burgess Ernest, and McKenzie Roderick. Chicago: University of Chicago Press.

Carlsson, Christoffer. 2012. "Using 'Turning Points' to Understand Processes of Change in Offending Notes from a Swedish Study on Life Courses and Crime." *British Journal of Criminology* 52 (1): 1–16.

Cohen, Albert Kircidel. 1955. *Delinquent Boys: The Culture of the Gang.* Glencoe, IL: Free Press.

Cohen, Cathy. 2004. "Deviance as Resistance." *Du Bois Review Social Science Research On Race* 1 (1): 27–45.

Duneier, Mitchell. 2000. *Sidewalk.* New York: Farrar, Straus and Giroux.

Durkheim, Emile. 1965. *The Elementary Forms of the Religious Life.* New York: Free Press.

Edin, Kathryn, and Maria Kefalas. 2005. *Promises I Can Keep: Why Poor Women Put Motherhood before Marriage.* Berkeley: University of California Press.

Edin, Kathryn, and Laura Lein. 1997. *Making Ends Meet: How Single Mothers Survive Welfare and Low Wage Work.* New York. Russel Sage Foundation.

Erikson, Erik H. 1994. *Identity: Youth and Crisis.* New York: W.W. Norton.

Estrada-Martinez, Lorena M., Cleopatra Howard Caldwell, Amy J. Schulz, Ana V. Diez-Roux, and Silvia Pedraza. 2013. "Families, Neighborhood Sociodemographic Factors, and Violent Behaviors among Latino, White, and Black Adolescents." *Youth and Society* 45 (2): 221–42.

Fader, Jamie. 2013. *Falling Back: Incarceration and Transitions to Adulthood among Urban Youth.* New Brunswick, NJ: Rutgers University Press.

Farmer, Richard F., and Alexander L. Chapman. 2008. *Behavioral Interventions in Cognitive Behavior Therapy: Practical Guidance for Putting Theory into Action.* Washington, DC: American Psychological Association.

Farrall, Stephen. 2005. "On the Existential Aspects of Desistance from Crime." *Symbolic Interaction* 28 (3): 367–86.

Farrington, David P., and Rolf Loeber. 2000. "Epidemiology of Juvenile Violence." *Child and Adolescent Psychiatric Clinics of North America* 9 (4): 733–48.

Feld, Barry C. 1999. *Bad Kids: Race and the Transformation of the Juvenile Court.* New York: Oxford University Press.

Felson, Marcus, and Lawrence E. Cohen. 1979. "Social Change and Crime Rate Trends: A Routine Activity Approach." *American Sociological Review* 44 (4): 588–608.

Foucault, Michel. 1995. *Discipline and Punish: The Birth of the Prison.* New York: Vintage.

———. 2005. *The Hermeneutics of the Subject: Lectures at the Collège de France, 1981–1982.* New York: Picador.

Gadd, David, and Stephen Farrall. 2004. "Criminal Careers, Desistance, and Subjectivity: Interpreting Men's Narratives of Change." *Theoretical Criminology* 8 (2): 123–56.

Gatti, Uberto, Richard E. Tremblay, and Frank Vitaro. 2009. "Latrogenic Effect of Juvenile Justice." *Journal of Child Psychology and Psychiatry* 50 (8): 991–98.

Gaventa, John. 1982. *Power and Powerlessness: Quiescence and Rebellion in an Appalachian Valley.* Urbana: University of Illinois Press.

Gerth, Hans, and C. Wright Mills, trans. and ed. 1946. *From Max Weber.* New York: Oxford University Press.

Giordano, Peggy C., Ryan D. Schroeder, and Stephen A. Cernkovich. 2007. "Emotions and Crime over the Life Course: A Neo-Meadian Perspective on Criminal Continuity and Change." *American Journal of Sociology* 112 (6): 1603–61.

Giordano, Peggy C., Stephen A. Cernkovich, and Jennifer L. Rudolph. 2002. "Gender, Crime, and Desistance: Toward a Theory of Cognitive Transformation." *American Journal of Sociology* 107 (4): 990–1064.

Goffman, Alice. 2014. *On the Run: Fugitive Life in an American City.* Chicago: University of Chicago Press.

Goffman, Erving. 1959. *The Presentation of Self in Everyday Life.* New York: Anchor Books.

———. 1986. *Frame Analysis: An Essay on the Organization of Experience.* Boston: Northeastern University Press.

Gottfredson, Michael R., and Travis Hirschi. 1990. *A General Theory of Crime.* Stanford, CA: Stanford University Press.

Haney, Lynne. 2010. *Offending Women: Power, Punishment, and the Regulation of Desire.* Berkeley: University of California Press.

Harcourt, Bernard E. 2006. *Language of the Gun: Youth, Crime, and Public Policy.* Chicago: University of Chicago Press.

Horowitz, Ruth. 1992. *Honor and the American Dream: Culture and Identity in a Chicano Community.* New Brunswick, NJ: Rutgers University Press.

Hunt, Morton. 1961. "How Does It Come to Be So?" *New Yorker* (January 28): 39–63.

Inderbitzin, Michelle. 2007a. "Inside a Maximum-Security Juvenile Training School: Institutional Attempts to Redefine the American Dream and to 'Normalize' Incarcerated Youth." *Punishment and Society* 9 (3): 235–51.

———. 2007b. "A Look from the Inside" Balancing Custody and Treatment in a Juvenile Maximum-Security Facility." *International Journal of Offender Therapy and Comparative Criminology* 51 (3): 348–62.

Jacobs, Mark D. 1993. *Screwing the System and Making It Work: Juvenile Justice in the No-Fault Society.* Chicago: University of Chicago Press.

Jerolmack, Colin, and Shamus Khan. 2014. "Talk Is Cheap: Ethnography and the Attitudinal Fallacy." *Sociological Methods and Research* 43 (2): 178–209.

Joas, Hans, and Wolfgang Knöbl. 2004. *Sozialtheorie Zwanzig Einführende Vorlesungen.* Frankfurt am Main, Germany: Suhrkamp.

Katz, Jack. 1988. *Seductions of Crime: Moral and Sensual Attractions in Doing Evil.* New York: Basic Books.

Khan, Shamus Rahman. 2011. *Privilege: The Making of an Adolescent Elite at St. Paul's School*. Princeton, NJ: Princeton University Press.

Kupchik, Aaron. 2006. *Judging Juveniles: Prosecuting Adolescents in Adult and Juvenile Courts*. New York: New York University Press.

Landenberger, Nana A., and Mark W. Lipsey. 2005. "The Positive Effects of Cognitive-Behavioral Programs for Offenders: A Meta-analysis of Factors Associated with Effective Treatment." *Journal of Experimental Criminology* 1 (4): 451–76.

Lareau, Annette. 2003. *Unequal Childhoods: Class, Race, and Family Life*. Berkeley: University of California Press.

Laub, John H., and Robert J. Sampson. 2003. *Shared Beginnings, Divergent Lives: Delinquent Boys to Age 70*. Cambridge, MA: Harvard University Press.

Laub, John, Daniel Nagin, and Robert Sampson. 1998. "Trajectories of Change in Criminal Offending: Good Marriages and the Desistance Process" *American Sociological Review* 63: 225–38.

Leverentz, Andrea M. 2014. *The Ex-Prisoner's Dilemma*. New Brunswick, NJ: Rutgers University Press.

Lincoln, Bruce. 1989. *Discourse and the Construction of Society: Comparative Studies of Myth, Ritual, and Classification*. New York: Oxford University Press.

Mack, Julian. 1909. "The Juvenile Court." *Harvard Law Review* 23 (2): 104–22.

MacLeod, Jay. 2008. *Ain't No Makin' It: Aspirations and Attainment in a Low-Income Neighborhood*. Boulder, CO: Westview Press.

Martin, Luther, Gutman Huck, and Patrick H. Hutton, eds. 1988. *Technologies of the Self: A Seminar with Michel Foucault*. Amherst: University of Massachusetts Press, 1988.

Maruna, Shadd. 2001. *Making Good: How Ex-convicts Reform and Rebuild Their Lives*. Washington, DC: American Psychological Association.

Maruna, Shadd, Louise Wilson, and Kathryn Curran. 2006. "Why God Is Often Found behind Bars: Prison Conversions and the Crisis of Self-Narrative." *Research in Human Development* 3 (2–3): 161–84.

Massey, Douglas, and Nancy Denton. 1993. *American Apartheid: Segregation and the Making of the Underclass*. Cambridge, MA: Harvard University Press.

Mazzei, Julie, and Erin E. O'Brien. 2009. "You Got It, So When Do You Flaunt It?" *Journal of Contemporary Ethnography* 38 (3): 358–83.

Mead, George Herbert. 1918. "The Psychology of Punitive Justice." *American Journal of Sociology* 23 (5): 577–602.

———. 1969. *Mind, Self, and Society*. Edited by Charles W. Morris. Chicago: University of Chicago Press.

Merton, Robert K. 1938. "Social Structure and Anomie." *American Sociological Review* 3 (5): 672–82.

Messner, Steven F., and Richard Rosenfeld. 2007. *Crime and the American Dream.* Belmont, CA: Wadsworth.

Pager, Devah. 2003. "The Mark of a Criminal Record." *American Journal of Sociology* 108 (5): 937–75.

Park, Robert. 1984. "The City: Suggestions for the Investigation of Human Behavior in the Urban Environment." In *The City*, 1–46. By Robert Park, Burgess Ernest, and McKenzie Roderick. Chicago: University of Chicago Press.

Pettit, Becky, and Bruce Western. 2004. "Mass Imprisonment and the Life Course: Race and Class Inequality in U.S. Incarceration." *American Sociological Review* 69 (2): 151–69.

Pattillo-McCoy, Mary. 1999. *Black Picket Fences: Privilege and Peril among the Black Middle Class.* Chicago: University of Chicago Press.

Piquero, Nicole L., and Miriam Sealock. 2010. "Race, Crime, and General Strain Theory." *Youth Violence and Juvenile Justice* 8 (3): 170–86.

Piven, Frances Fox, and Richard A. Cloward. 1993. *Regulating the Poor: The Function of Public Welfare.* New York: Vintage.

Platt, Anthony M. 1977. *The Child Savers: The Invention of Delinquency.* 2nd ed. Chicago: University of Chicago Press.

Quinn, Ashley, and Wes Shera. 2009. "Evidence-Based Practice in Group Work with Incarcerated Youth." *International Journal of Law and Psychiatry* 32 (5): 288–93.

Reich, Adam. 2010. *Hidden Truth: Young Men Navigating Lives in and out of Juvenile Prison.* Berkeley: University of California Press.

Rios, Victor M. 2011. *Punished: Policing the Lives of Black and Latino Boys.* New York: New York University Press.

Rothman, David J. 2008. *The Discovery of the Asylum: Social Order and Disorder in the New Republic.* New Jersey: Transaction.

Sampson, Robert, and John H. Laub. 1993. "Structural Variations in Juvenile Court Processing: Inequality, the Underclass, and Social Control." *Law and Society Review* 27 (2): 285–311.

———. 2005. "A Life-Course View of the Development of Crime." *Annals of the American Academy of Political and Social Science* 602: 12–45.

Schlossman, Steven L. 2005. *Transforming Juvenile Justice: Reform, Ideals, and Institutional Realities, 1825–1920.* DeKalb: Northern Illinois University Press.

Scott, James C. 1987. *Weapons of the Weak: Everyday Forms of Peasant Resistance.* New Haven: Yale University Press.

———. 1992. *Domination and the Arts of Resistance: Hidden Transcripts.* New Haven: Yale University Press.

Sewell, William H. 1992. "A Theory of Structure: Duality, Agency, and Transformation." *American Journal of Sociology* 98 (1): 1–29.

———. 2011. *The Philosophy of Money.* Edited by David Frisby. Translated by Tom Bottomore. New York: Routledge.

Simmel, Georg. 2011 [1900]. *Philosophy of Money.* Translated by Tom Bottomore and David Frisby. Foreword by Charles Lemert. New York: Routledge, 2011.

———. 1971 [1908]. The Stranger. In *Individuality and Social Forms,* 143–49. Edited by Donald N. Levine. Chicago: University of Chicago Press, 1971.

Sorkin, Andrew Ross, and Megan Thee-Brenan. 2014. "Many Feel the American Dream Is Out of Reach Poll Shows." *New York Times* (November 12). http://dealbook.nytimes.com/2014/12/10/many-feel-the-american-dream-is-out-of-reach-poll-shows/. Accessed March 26, 2016.

Soss, Joe, Richard C. Fording, and Sanford F. Schram. 2011. *Disciplining the Poor: Neoliberal Paternalism and the Persistent Power of Race.* Chicago: University of Chicago Press.

Stack, Carol B. 1974. *All Our Kin: Strategies for Survival in a Black Community.* New York: Basic Books.

Swidler, Ann. 1986. "Culture in Action: Symbols and Strategies." *American Sociological Review* 51 (2): 273–86.

Tucker, Robert C., ed. 1978. *The Marx-Engels Reader.* 2nd ed. New York: W. W. Norton.

Uggen, Christopher. 2000. "Work as a Turning Point in the Life Course of Criminals: A Duration Model of Age, Employment, and Recidivism." *American Sociological Review* 65: 529–46.

Vaughan, Barry. 2007. "The Internal Narrative of Desistance." *British Journal of Criminology* 47 (3): 390–404.

Venkatesh, Sudhir Alladi. 2002. *American Project: The Rise and Fall of a Modern Ghetto.* Cambridge, MA: Harvard University Press.

———. 2008. *Gang Leader for a Day: A Rogue Sociologist Takes to the Streets.* New York: Penguin Press.

Wacquant, Loïc. 2005. "Carnal Connections: On Embodiment, Apprenticeship, and Membership." *Qualitative Sociology* 28 (4): 445–74.

———. 2006. *Body and Soul: Notebooks of an Apprentice Boxer.* New York: Oxford University Press.

———. 2008. "The Place of the Prison in the New Government of Poverty." In *After the War on Crime: Race, Democracy, and a New Reconstruction,* 23–36. Edited by Mary Frampton et al. New York: New York University Press.

Wakefield, Sarah, and Christopher Uggen. 2010. Incarceration and Stratification. *Annual Review of Sociology* 36 (1): 387–406.

Weber, Max. 1949. *Max Weber on the Methodology of the Social Sciences*. Edited and translated by Edward A. Shils and Henry A. Finch. Glencoe, IL: Free Press.

———. 1958. *From Max Weber: Essays in Sociology*. Edited and translated by Hans H. Gerth and Charles Wright Mills. New York: Oxford University Press.

———. 1979. *Economy and Society: An Outline of Interpretive Sociology*. Edited by Guenther Roth and Claus Wittich. Translated by Ephraim Fischoff et al. Berkeley: University of California Press.

———. (1904–5) 2002. *The Protestant Ethic and the Spirit of Capitalism: And Other Writings*. Translated by Peter Baehr and Gordon C. Wells. New York: Penguin Classics.

Western, Bruce. 2006. *Punishment and Inequality in America*. New York: Russell Sage Foundation.

Willis, Paul. 1981. *Learning to Labor. How Working Class Kids Get Working Class Jobs*. New York: Columbia University Press.

Wilson, William Julius. 1990. *The Truly Disadvantaged: The Inner City, the Underclass, and Public Policy*. Chicago: University Of Chicago Press.

———. 2009. *More Than Just Race: Being Black and Poor in the Inner City*. New York: W. W. Norton.

Wu, Boshiu, Stephen Cernovich, and Christopher Dunn. 1997. "Assessing the Effects of Race and Class on Juvenile Justice Processing in Ohio." *Journal of Criminal Justice* 25 (4): 265–77.

Young, Alford. *The Mind of Marginalized Black Men*. Princeton, NJ: Princeton University Press, 2006.

Zimring, Franklin E. 2005. *American Juvenile Justice*. Oxford: Oxford University Press.

Zelizer, Viviana. 1997. *The Social Meaning of Money: Pin Money, Paychecks, Poor Relief, and Other Currencies*. Princeton, NJ: Princeton University Press.

Index